CHRISTMAS STITCHES

CHRISTMAS STITCHES

GAIL HARKER

WARD LOCK

This book is dedicated to all my grandchildren. To those who are with us now – Lindsay, Amanda, Zeke, Eddie – and to those who have yet to appear. Also, to dear friends around the world with whom many a joyful Christmas has been spent: Gerda and Chris Howard, Chloe and Doug Percy, and Colleen and Bill Philliber.

First published in the UK 1996
by Cassell
Wellington House
125 Strand
LONDON
WC2R 0BB

Distributed in the United States
by Sterling Publishing Co., Inc.
387 Park Avenue South, New York, NY 10016-8810

Designed by Isobel Gillan
Illustrated by Nicola Gregory from original designs by Gail Harker
Charts by Jenny Dooge
Photographed by Ed Barber

A British Library Cataloguing in Publication Data block for this book may be obtained from the British Library

ISBN 0 304 34596 2

Printed and bound in Spain by Bookprint

CONTENTS

THE PROJECTS

THE TASSELS

INTRODUCTION

Christmas marks the middle of the winter season, punctuated with gloomy, cold weather for many of those people who live in Europe and America. Ever since man began to take notice of the seasons and the progress of stars and planets across the heavens, the celebration of mid-winter has been a vital part of human existence. Winter solstice celebrations continue amongst some of the most ancient societies.

The birth of the Christ Child ushered in the whole Christian era. The celebration of Christ's nativity has been fraught with questions about the exact time and place of the event. For most, those details are less important than the idea behind the occasion – the concept of peace on earth and good will to all proves irresistible. The season that has a growing universal appeal throughout the world brings together families and friends. Yuletide has seen the development of traditions from many cultures which have cross fertilized all they touch, linking peoples in common celebration.

American Christmas traditions owe much to those of Britain, which, in turn, owe much to the German traditions brought to Britain by Prince Albert. Most families develop their own ways of celebrating the birth of the Christ Child. The extent of those celebrations has grown to immense proportions over the years. Homes are now extensively decorated, helping to communicate the joy of the season. Presents for family and friends are gaily decorated with brightly coloured paper, ribbons and glitter. This book is devoted such to gifts and decorations, containers, bags and baubles, which can be made by anyone, of any skill level. The beauty of such personal gifts, made by loving hands, is that they reflect and communicate the real spirit of Christmas.

PROJECT GUIDELINES

FABRICS

All the projects in this book specify the type of fabric required to work them. Fabrics can vary tremendously and some effects rely upon specific fabric qualities. For most of the projects, only small quantities of fabric (and thread) are needed. Where substitutions can be made, they have been noted in each project. Some fabrics are known by different names in different markets throughout the world. For this reason, they have been described by their unique qualities, to make it easier to find the exact material or one that is similar.

Most fabrics can be found in general fabric shops, but some may only be available from specialist shops catering to bridal requisites, specialist sewing, or embroidery materials. Individual projects may use a wide variety of materials. If it is not possible to find the specified fabric look for a substitute with similar characteristics.

Cotton and cotton prints. At Christmas time sewing shops are filled with fabrics covered by Christmas patterns, designs, and themes. Start looking for them from September onwards.

Canvas and other embroidery fabrics. Canvas for canvas work is widely available from embroidery shops. It can also be found in general merchandise or wool shops. The number of threads per inch of weave is referred to as gauge, and the gauge varies depending on how close together the weft and warp threads are woven. The size of the gauge will affect the appearance and size of the finished work. Canvas is further defined by the way in which it is woven and whether or not it has one or more threads in the mesh. A single thread mesh is known as mono or single mesh. Two thread mesh is described as double mesh. All projects in this book use mono canvas.

Even weave fabrics. Cotton or linen even weave fabrics are specifically used by embroiderers. They all have threads which can be easily counted, both horizontally and vertically. These fabrics are also defined by the number of threads per inch in the weave. The embroiderer works patterns over these fabrics in a manner similar to canvas work.

Glittery and see-through fabrics. The Christmas season has a great affinity with glittery, sparkling fabrics and threads, with fabric shops well stocked with them at this festive time of the year. Some of the projects are worked with fused layers of these fabrics, one on top of the other. Keep a look-out for scraps of lightweight, diaphanous, or see-through, fabrics, which can be used to create three-

dimensional embroidered effects. Nylon organza or
net is made to simulate silk organza and net, but is
much cheaper to buy and is more resistant to fraying.

Jumble or rummage sales can sometimes be the
source of remarkable finds. Be aware of those little
glints that seem to jump out at you. Keep a large
glass jar or two to store almost-used reels of thread,
ribbons, cord and tiny scraps of fabric. This treasure
trove will provide the inspiration for many
wonderful Christmas creations. Almost any thin
fabric, natural or synthetic, can be used for fused
appliqué projects.

Non-woven fabrics. Non-woven fabrics will not
fray. Fabrics in this category are felt, leather, and
some synthetics. Tassels can be made from felt. Felt is
a good stitching medium and can be used for all
sorts of decorations embellished with glittering
thread or beads. The hanging heart frame (page 84)
could also be made from felt. Very thin metallic-
looking lamé works well for tassels and fused
decorations, although it is prone to fraying.

Wadding. There are many types of wadding
available, ranging from thick to thin, and in natural
or synthetic fibres. Needle punched cotton wadding
is thin, light and easy to work. Use it for the
Christmas rose photo frame (page 78), and
Christmas tree skirt (page 90). If this wadding is not
available, look for the lightweight, thin, blanket-like
material, or acrylic wadding. Quilter's shops are a
good source for these materials.

Fusible webbing. This is another product with
different names in different markets. Supplied in a
variety of weights it can be employed to apply one
fabric to another, using heat. It is protected on one
side by a backing paper which allows separate
bonding to each side. Always read the manufacturer's
instructions and remember to test a small sample
before committing to the finished piece, as some
fabrics may react unpredictably. Make sure that thin
or transparent fabrics do not burn when the heat is
applied. A lightweight webbing is used in the
glittering decorations project (page 24).

Pelmet Vilene (UK), Timtex (USA). This is the
heaviest non-woven material. It was developed for
use in making soft furnishings such as curtain
headings, belts, and hat brim stiffeners. It is available
in both narrow and wide widths, and intended to
provide maximum fabric stiffness. It is very adaptable
and can be used unframed, for machine embroidery
and with automatic machine stitches. It can also be
used to make the glittering decorations (page 24)
and for the hanging heart photo frame (page 84). It
can be worked with metallic braid and by hand with
a crewel or chenille needle. Use a 14/90 or 16/100
machine needle with this material.

Fabric stabilizer. This prevents fabric from
puckering while decorative stitches are being
applied by machine. Slip a piece under the fabric,
stitch through the fabric, turn the fabric over and
carefully tear off the stabilizer. There are many types
on the market.

Iron-on interfacings. These are non-woven
products and are available in a variety of weights.
They have a pebbly surface on the side that is fused
to another material. They are used for stiffening and
the extra firmness helps when machine stitching,
preventing fabric puckering.

Polyester stuffing or toy stuffing. Use to stuff all
canvas work decorations.

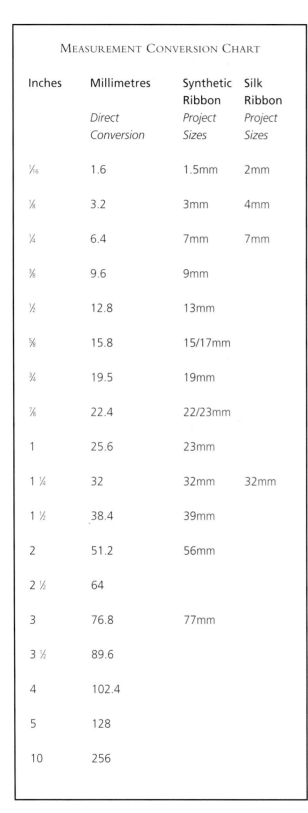

MEASUREMENT CONVERSION CHART			
Inches	Millimetres	Synthetic Ribbon	Silk Ribbon
	Direct Conversion	*Project Sizes*	*Project Sizes*
1/16	1.6	1.5mm	2mm
1/8	3.2	3mm	4mm
1/4	6.4	7mm	7mm
3/8	9.6	9mm	
1/2	12.8	13mm	
5/8	15.8	15/17mm	
3/4	19.5	19mm	
7/8	22.4	22/23mm	
1	25.6	23mm	
1 1/4	32	32mm	32mm
1 1/2	38.4	39mm	
2	51.2	56mm	
2 1/2	64		
3	76.8	77mm	
3 1/2	89.6		
4	102.4		
5	128		
10	256		

RIBBONS

Ribbons are supplied in a wide variety of widths, fabrics, patterns, and colours. They are sold in metric sizes as well as inches, or Imperial measure. To cut through some of the resulting confusion, the conversion chart on the left will help you to make adjustments. Ribbons are available from department stores, wherever sewing goods are sold, or at specialist embroidery shops.

If ribbons are only sold in inches, and directions indicate metric sizes, use the conversion to look up the metric size and read across to the inch equivalent. If directions indicate inch measurements and ribbons are only available in metric sizes, look up the Imperial measurement, and read across to the metric equivalent.

Most manufacturers will supply a full catalogue of their wares, sometimes for a fee. If you cannot find the ribbon you want, be creative and make your own. Cut fabric straight into strips about 1/2 in (1.25 cm) wider than you need, turn the edges under and press them flat, then use as required.

Silk ribbon. When stitching, silk ribbons act quite differently from synthetic ones. The soft, pliable nature of the silk allows it to be easily worked in hand embroidery. Silk ribbons are used in the Christmas rose photo frame project (page 78). Both silk and synthetic ribbon could be used to fold and turn to create the roses. The Christmas rose cushion (page 74) uses this technique. Synthetic fabric ribbons, have been used to make several of the tassels (page 120).

Wired ribbon. This ribbon has wires running along both edges. These ribbons hold their shape when bent, and will not sag. They may be used to make gathered roses or bows. Synthetic ribbons have been used for making several of the tassels (page 109) and in the Christmas star project (page 28), for the prairie points.

RIBBON WORK STITCHES

Straight stitch. Bring the ribbon-threaded needle up at point (A). Smooth the ribbon out over the fabric and reinsert the needle at a point along any proposed design line (B). Push the needle through both ribbon and fabric. Ease the ribbon through to the back, allowing it to curl slightly (C).

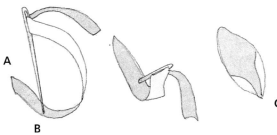

French knot. Bring the ribbon-threaded needle to the right side of the fabric. Wrap the ribbon once around the needle, taking the needle back through the fabric a short distance from the original point. Do not pull the stitch too tightly.

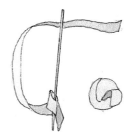

Chain stitch. Push the needle in and out of the fabric, looping the thread or ribbon under the needle as you do so. On the second stitch, insert the needle at the front of the previous loop. Work seven or eight chain stitches in a spiral around the French knot to create a rose effect. Leave the ribbon loose to create a puffed effect.

THREADS FOR HAND EMBROIDERY

There is a wide variety of threads on the market manufactured from a range of fibres such as cotton, wool, rayon, silk, linen, synthetics, and metal. Mercerised thread is cotton treated to strengthen it, make it shiny and susceptible to dye. Use the care and cleaning instructions from the information supplied by the manufacturer. Commonly available embroidery threads are as follows:

Six-stranded cotton. A lustrous, 100% mercerised cotton thread available in about four hundred colours. The lightly twisted strands are supplied in skeins. All six strands can be used together, or they can be split into one or more threads. Stranded cotton works well for tassels and cords.

DMC perlé. A mercerised cotton thread with a very shiny finish and a pronounced twist, supplied in skeins. DMC perlé is supplied in sizes 3, 5, 8, and 12. The smaller the number, the thicker the thread. This thread has been recommended to use for the poinsettia book covers (page 62), some of the cords (page 40), and the buttonhole napkin rings (page 36). When used for stitching, an embossed effect is produced. This thread cannot be split.

Cotton à broder. A very lightly twisted, soft-looking, single cotton thread with some sheen. This thread is used in buttonhole rings (page 36), for tassels (page 109) and hand stitching.

Soft embroidery cotton. A fairly thick, 5 ply, soft cotton thread with a matte finish. It can not be split. It is used to make tassels and cords.

Silk thread. This is available as stranded or twisted thread and has a high sheen. Silk stranded thread may be used instead of stranded cotton.

Crewel wool. A fine, twisted wool, 2 ply thread used in crewel, canvas work and other stitching.

Space-dyed or over-dyed threads. These are specially dyed in a range of colours on the same thread. A single thread has many colours appearing irregularly spaced along the length of the thread. These threads give a varied appearance when worked. They are available at speciality needlework shops and by mail order from specialist outlets.

Synthetic threads. There is an increasing volume of all types of synthetic fibre thread coming on to the market. Their characteristics are different from natural fibre threads and it is sometimes necessary to take special considerations when stitching, as synthetic threads are springier than natural ones.

Kreinik metallic braid. These smooth, round threads may not sound as if they would be good candidates for stitching, but they create wonderful, glittery results. The metallic braids are supplied in various weights (8 fine, 16 medium, 32 heavy), which makes them useful for a range of stitching techniques. Several of the projects suggest using metallic braids. They are used on edges of tablecloths, napkins, and for the hanging heart photo frame (page 84).

Synthetic metallics. These threads have the same use as non-metallics and can be substituted one for the other. To do this, determine that the thread will fill the hole in the canvas without crowding the surrounding threads. The thread should not shred or fall apart while it is being worked, and you should be able to pull it through the fabric without too much resistance. These threads produce a very nice effect. Experiment with a few skeins to determine how and where to use them.

THREADS FOR MACHINE EMBROIDERY

Most threads are developed for specific purposes. Dressmaker's threads are manufactured with a high twist which contributes to their strength and durability. But, when applied, they do not spread and show off their colour and lustre. On the other hand, machine embroidery threads do not have a high twist, and are therefore not as strong. However, they spread nicely on the fabric as they are applied, showing off their lovely colour and sheen.

Machine embroidery threads are supplied by a number of manufacturers in a wide range of fibres. They could be made of cotton, rayon, silk, fibre blends, or metallics. Be sure to use standard dressmaker's threads for making up projects or for general sewing.

Threads are supplied in a range of sizes, 50 is thin, and 30 is an intermediate thickness. Some threads may not be numbered, but will be identified as machine embroidery thread. These threads are used in the hanging heart photo frame (page 84), tablecloth edges (page 104), and for tassel making.

TIPS FOR MACHINE STITCHING METALLIC AND THICKER THREADS

When heavier or thicker threads are used, work with a 14/90 or a 16/100 needle. Also, reduce your machine's top tension slightly. Use a special embroidery needle, or Metafil needle, for metallic threads. The top stitch needle will also accommodate thicker threads.

NEEDLES FOR HAND STITCHING

Needles are available in numerous types, with each type available in a range of sizes. Sizes are classified by gauge, length and size of the eye. Large needles are identified by smaller numbers with the smallest needles having the largest numbers. For those who find it difficult to thread a needle with embroidery threads, try using a needle threader. Alternatively, cut a narrow strip of paper, fold it in half, place the thread in the fold, and pull it through the eye. Re-cutting the thread with sharp scissors may also help to thread a difficult strand.

Which Needle To Use

Stitchers require a selection of needles. The size of the eye of the needle will vary depending on the type of needle and purpose for which it was designed. A thick thread will obviously not go through a tiny eye. On the other hand, a needle that is too large could distort or tear the fabric or canvas on which it is used. A tapestry needle, for instance, should not be used for other embroidery. The blunt point will not pierce the fabric. Use these needles only on fabric that has a pronounced hole or space in the weave. (★ denotes needles specified in projects)

Embroidery/crewel★. These have sharp points with long eyes to allow you to pass one or more threads through the eye. They are the most commonly used needle for surface embroidery. They are used to work the edgings on the buttonhole napkin rings (page 36).

Sharps. Have sharp points and are used for general sewing, patchwork, quilting and making up projects.

Chenille★. Have sharp points and are good for stitching coarse materials with thick yarns.

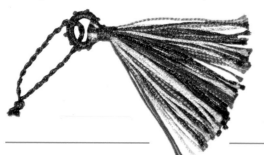

Darning. Large darning needles (sometimes long) with sharp points and a large eye are used for stitching thick fabric.

Betweens/quilting★. Have sharp points and are designed for short, quick, even stitching. They are invaluable to quilters.

Tapestry. Have blunt, rounded points with large, long eyes to accommodate wool and heavier yarns. They are designed to slip between threads rather than splitting through them. Good for use on even weave fabrics and for canvas work decorations. They can also be used to thread cords on the little gift bags (page 56).

Beading. A very long, thin needle designed specifically to use for threading beads, but not practical for every project.

Bodkin★. Have blunt points and may be flat or round. They have a large eye which makes them good for threading cords. Bodkins are also used for darning. This implement is handy for threading cords on the little gift bags (page 56).

You will often need a heavier needle to accommodate blended fibres or twisted metal threads. You may find that you need a larger needle than specified on a project. A 14/90 needle is suggested for the hanging hearts (page 84) but a larger needle may be required. For difficult threads, a top stitch, embroidery, or Metafil needle may help.

MACHINE EMBROIDERY NEEDLES									
English	8	9	10	11	12	14	16	18	20
Continental	60	65	70	75	80	90	100	110	120
	Very Fine			*Medium*				*Very Heavy*	

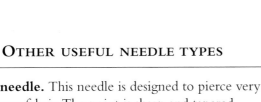

OTHER USEFUL NEEDLE TYPES

Jeans needle. This needle is designed to pierce very stiff, dense fabric. The point is sharp and tapered. The needle is good for stitching heavy fabrics and for interfacings.

Top stitch needle. This is a special design with a very large eye. The needle accommodates heavier threads, or allows two threads to be used in the needle at one time.

EMBROIDERY ACCESSORIES

Pin cushion. Have a pin cushion within easy reach. It will keep needles safe, accessible, and some have a special filling to prevent rust.

Scissors and knives. You will need small, sharp scissors for all embroidery projects. A craft knife or rotary cutter and steel rule may also be handy. Keep them out of the reach of children.

Embroidery hoops or frames. The majority of projects in this book are small. However, it is sometimes necessary to use an embroidery hoop or frame to hold the fabric taut so that it does not distort when it is worked. Alternatively you could fasten the work in a picture frame, or on painter's canvas stretchers. Use drawing pins to secure the work. To work book marks or to attach buttons, sequins, and beads, secure the fabric in a small frame.

MACHINE EMBROIDERY

No matter how complex your machine or how humble, most will provide interesting patterns you could use for the projects in this book.

Automatic stitches and patterns. Automatic stitches are worked with the presser foot attached to the machine. They are accessed by pressing a button, inserting a cam, or by a computer screen selection.

Some manufacturers label these stitches as utility or decorative stitches, especially if they are designed for a particular function. Sometimes, a special foot is provided for these stitches. The most basic machine will almost certainly provide a few stitch options. In all cases, check your machine manual for instructions to familiarize yourself with its capabilities and limitations. When working automatic stitches on fabric, always support dense stitching with a backing fabric such as Vilene, Timtex or stabilizer.

Try out the stitches that are available on your machine and become familiar with all the possibilities. Use machine embroidery threads to work stitches, as using a heavier dressmaker's thread for automatic stitch patterns may prevent the machine from working properly.

Machine preparation. Ensure that top thread and bobbin thread are balanced: the two threads lock in the centre of the fabric being stitched. Test your machine using different thread colours for top and bottom. Sew a few stitches, and check to see that the bobbin thread colour does not show on the top of the fabric. Turn the fabric over to check that the top thread is not showing on the bottom of the fabric.

Adjusting balance. If the bobbin thread shows on the top of the fabric there are two possible remedies. Reduce the top tension until it no longer shows on top of the fabric, or gradually increase the bobbin tension until the thread no longer shows on the top.

Most machines have a top tension indicator dial with a knob or lever with which you can make adjustments. The scale will usually run from 0 to 10. For general sewing, the dial will probably rest between 4 and 5. To reduce the top tension you should reduce the number setting. Some machines merely indicate top tension as a plus (+) or minus (-). To reduce the tension, move the dial towards the minus sign.

When the thread tension has been balanced for straight stitch, it may need to be changed for zig-zag or other automatic patterns. If so, adjust following the above instructions. It does not matter if top thread shows slightly on the underside of the fabric unless both sides of the finished work will be visible.

TRANSFERRING DESIGNS TO FABRIC

Always make faint lines with a special marker like the ones below. Big bold lines may be hard to remove when they are not even meant to be seen. Use a light dashed, dotted, or broken line.

Tailor's or dressmaker's pencils. These are supplied as pencils or as wedges of chalk-like material. The marking medium may be brushed off the fabric after designs have been stitched. Pencil-type markers allow greater accuracy when marking.

Air-soluble felt tip marker. A variety of these products is available. These markers make a blue or purple line which fades away after a short period. Their performance varies depending upon the manufacturer and the fabric used. Always test with a trial sample.

Water-soluble felt tip marker. Use these to draw your design directly on to the fabric and then erase the lines after the stitches have been worked. One end of the marker has a drawing point, and the other an eraser. If you have a marker without an eraser, use a water-moistened cotton-tipped swab to remove lines. Test on your fabric before using.

Pencil. Use a hard lead pencil, such as a 4H.

ENLARGING OR REDUCING DESIGNS

Photocopier enlargement. There are a number of practical ways to enlarge designs, patterns, or templates. One of the easiest is by using a photocopier. You can use most office or home photocopiers to produce enlargements and reductions of a specified size.

MISCELLANEOUS MATERIALS

Spray enamel or florist's spray. These paints can be used on buttons, rings, beads, and other materials that you would like to be a different colour. They are readily available from art supply shops, D.I.Y. shops, and craft supply shops. Auto supply stores will always have car spray enamels which are perfectly suitable. Read the instructions and use with care.

Clothes pins or pegs. These devices make wonderful little clamps. Use them when making tassels. Craft shops sell tiny clothes pins, smaller than the laundry type, that are often very handy to use.

Wire twist-ties. These are used to secure plastic bags. The little paper-covered wires make useful holding devices.

Craft board. This is thick card, cardboard, foam board or similar board that can be used with pins. It is useful for pinning down tassels and other items while working on them.

T-pins. Handy for use where pins are inserted and moved as the work progresses. They are also useful for pinning cords or tassels. Quilting pins could also be used.

Buttons, beads, rings. These are often available from jumble sales, in boxes, or jam jars, in assorted sizes, and shapes. New ones are available from needlecraft or fabric shops. Paint them in a suitable colour using spray enamel or florist's spray, or sort them into colour groups. Rings can be a variety of sizes ranging from ¾in (2cm) to 2in (5cm) in diameter. Rings could be plastic, any non-corrosive metal, or bolt washers. Look for anything suitable with a hole in the middle.

Hardware. The D.I.Y. shops will become friendly haunts of many project workers. Here you can find wonderful small hardware items including washers, 'O' rings, plastic rings, curtain rings, brass products, cadmium-coated products, and other items providing instant inspiration.

Thread reels or spools. Empty spools and reels offer great potential for tassel heads and other festive decorations.

Christmas paraphernalia. All sorts of decorative items may be used. Attach them to tassels, decorations, and all manner of decorative devices.

Fabric stiffener. There are a number of products used to stiffen fabrics. They include glues, wallpaper paste, laundry starch, specially designed commercial products, and blind stiffener. Stiffener has been used for the origami projects (page 30). Read the directions carefully and always follow the instructions. Where products without directions for stiffening fabric are used, thoroughly coat the fabric, scrape off the excess stiffener, lay the fabric out flat, and let it dry naturally. Natural fabrics accept stiffener best, but other fibres will also accept it.

After the fabrics have been treated and dried, they may be worked and used as if they were light card or heavy paper. Use rotary cutters, craft knives or scissors to cut shapes or patterns. Use a 'T' square or straight edge for accuracy where it is required. The origami decorations (page 30) and bags (page 52) are made from stiffened fabric. Fabrics treated in this way will accept both machine and hand stitching. It is advisable to use a large machine needle.

Cotton or tissue balls. These products are purpose-made for tassel heads. The tissue balls are made from compressed tissue. The balls come in a variety of sizes and will allow a needle to pass easily through them.

STITCHES FOR CANVAS WORK AND EVEN WEAVE

Specific stitches required to work canvas work and even weave projects are explained here and shown with step-by-step instructions.

CANVAS WORK STITCHES

Tent stitch. This is a stitch with many variations. The stitch, usually worked top to bottom, is also called continental stitch. The example shows the first row completed and turned so the second row can be worked. The work, after completing the first row, is turned end for end. The needle passes diagonally over one cross of canvas threads, and then diagonally behind two horizontal canvas threads.

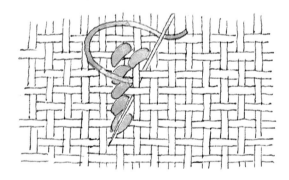

Horizontal tent stitch/continental stitch. Work first row from right to left (A). The needle passes diagonally over one cross of the canvas threads and then travels diagonally under two vertical canvas threads. This makes one stitch. To change from first to second row, insert the needle vertically under a horizontal canvas thread (B). This completes the last stitch on the preceding row and positions the needle to begin the next row of stitches. To work the

second row, either continue working from the left to right across the work (C), or rotate the canvas 180° (end for end) and work, as before, from right to left. This stitch looks long and slanted on the wrong side of the canvas.

A

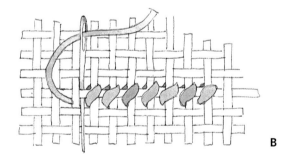

B

C

Diagonal tent stitch. This is also called basket weave. This stitch is worked either from top to bottom, or bottom to top. After the first diagonal row is worked, the second row is worked between the first row of stitches. The needle passes diagonally over one cross of the canvas threads from (A) to (B), and then horizontally behind two vertical canvas threads to (C) to create one stitch. The back of the canvas has the look of basket weave and makes a very durable piece of work.

Split stitch. This is a standard embroidery stitch worked in a similar fashion on canvas. Work the first row from left to right beginning at point (A). From point (A) take the needle, bottom to top, over four horizontal canvas threads to point (B), and return to the hole (C) next to point (A). Finish off the row in this fashion. To begin the second row, count down two horizontal canvas threads from the bottom of the first row of stitches. Bring the needle up at point (D) and back down through the stitch above, at point (E), splitting the thread of the previously made stitch with the needle. Continue working in this fashion until the row is completed.

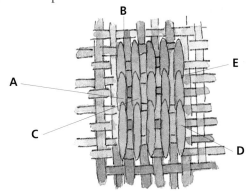

French knots. This is a standard stitch worked in canvas work exactly the same way it is worked for other embroidery. Bring the needle and thread up through one hole in the canvas. Wrap the thread a single turn around the needle and take it back down though an adjacent hole.

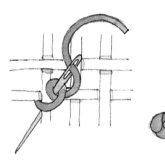

Mosaic stitch. This is a standard stitch. It is made up of a combination of three diagonal stitches. When this stitch is repeated, it takes on the appearance of tiles of stitches, hence the name mosaic. These tiles of stitches when used around the edge of a piece of work, make wonderful border patterns and create pleasing textural effects for filling in design areas.

Work from left to right, then right to left, making two journeys to complete each set of tiles. Come through the canvas at point (A) and cross one thread diagonally to point (B). Come down diagonally under two horizontal threads to point (C), then over two threads to point (D). Bring the needle vertically under one thread to point (E), then diagonally to point (F). Continue in this way to the end of the row.

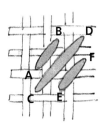

EVEN WEAVE STITCHES

Straight stitch. This stitch is primarily used to outline design shapes. It will help to emphasize the

shapes in those areas. It will often share a hole with another stitch. Do not make each stitch too long.

Satin stitch. Worked on even weave fabric this stitch is the same as conventional satin stitch, commonly used throughout the needlework world. For these designs, however, you count the warp and weft threads of the fabric to place your stitches, following the stitch chart. The needle is always worked through a space between the fabric's warp and weft threads. The stitch should fill the fabric without crowding adjacent stitches. Avoid putting too much tension on the embroidery thread as this will distort the fabric; keep the stitches short. Sometimes, two stitches will share the same space or hole. When this occurs, take the needle down to the back, from the front of the fabric, rather than up to the front, from the back.

To work satin stitch, make the stitches vertically or

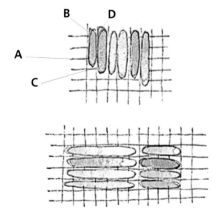

horizontally straight on the canvas from point (A) to point (B), then to point (C) and point (D) and so on.
Running stitch. This stitch is worked in a straight line, moving the needle in and out of the holes of the fabric.

Backstitch. This is used for edging other areas of stitching, or for a firm seam if hand stitching fabrics together. Work small, even stitches, inserting the needle along the sewing line behind where the thread emerges, then coming up again an equal distance beyond the thread.

Buttonhole stitch. Buttonhole stitch can be used as a filler stitch, but is more usually worked along the edge of a piece as a decoration or to finish a raw edge. The stiches are generally worked very close together. If they are more widely spaced, it is sometimes called a blanket stitch. Working from left to right along the fabric edge, insert the needle a short distance into the fabric and bring the needle out under the edge, threading the loop of thread as you do so.

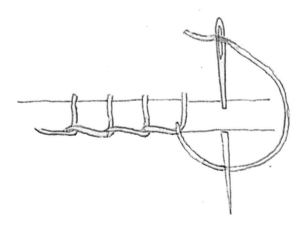

Detached buttonhole stitch. This is worked in the same way as buttonhole stitch, but working in a spiral around a tassel head, for example, and using the previous row of stitches as the base for the following row.

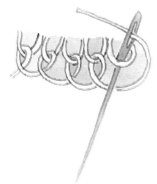

Detached chain stitch. Follow the instructions for simple chain stitch under Ribbon work stitches on page 11. To make a detached chain stitch, simply push the needle down through the fabric to hold and isolate each chain.

Cross stitch. There are a number of ways of working rows of cross stitch, but the important element is that the top diagonal stitch must always fall in the same direction, unless you particularly want a change in texture. The most common method is to work a row of diagonals in one direction, then return back over the row to complete the stitches.

ORGANISING A CANVAS WORK PROJECT

Stitch guide. It is always helpful to photocopy the stitch guide. It will lie flat and be easy to use while stitching. After you've bought all the necessary threads, cut a short piece from each and tape it to the corresponding position on the stitch guide. This should help prevent you working the wrong thread in any designated area.

Fabric edges. To prevent the fabric fraying along the edges, work a straight stitch, or narrow zig-zag, along the edges in a matching thread.

Framing the canvas. Use an embroidery frame for all the projects (page 15). This will help to keep the work flat and even. Do not cut out the project from the canvas until all stitching has been worked.
Stitching order. A stitching order is suggested to help simplify the process.

Acceptable thread substitutions. Where threads are specified you can substitute two strands of madeira or DMC cotton in place of two strands of DMC medici thread. Five strands of DMC stranded cotton may be used in place of medium weight Kreinik 16 metallic braid. Choose a matching colour to the one specified.

THE
PROJECTS

GLITTERING DECORATIONS

These dazzling decorations are made by fusing layers of brightly coloured fabric, thread, sequins and bits of decorative scrap materials. The fusing process stiffens the fabric, making it hold its own shape. The colours will become muted after they have been layered with a top layer of sheer fabric.

YOU WILL NEED

- [ ] felt or pelmet Vilene (UK), Timtex (USA) 8in (20cm) square
- [ ] lightweight fusible webbing 2 x 8in (20cm) square
- [ ] lamé or other thin fabric 8in (20cm) square
- [ ] assortment of sparkling, glitzy fabric, thread, sequins and glitter 8in (20cm) square
- [ ] sheer fabric 8in (20cm) square
- [ ] greaseproof parchment
- [ ] Kreinik 16 metallic braid, cable or ⅛in (3mm) ribbon, or DMC perlé 5 or 8
- [ ] beads, bells and sequins
- [ ] copier paper
- [ ] dressmaker's thread
- [ ] sharp needle
- [ ] scissors
- [ ] pencil
- [ ] fabric marker

If working on an intricately shaped decoration, try using a stiffer fabric, such as pelmet Vilene, instead of felt, as the basic background layer, as it will be easier to manipulate.

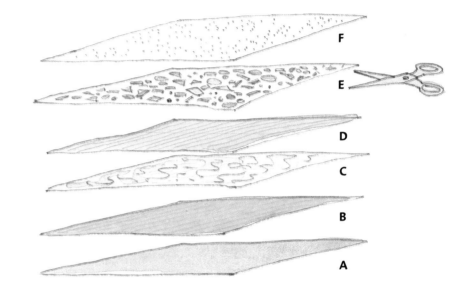

1 Layering and fusing fabric. Working from the bottom, layer your fabric one on top of the other step by step. You'll find more about fusing on page 9. Start with a piece of felt (A). On this, place a layer of fusible webbing, sticky-side down (B), and a sheet of greaseproof parchment to prevent the material sticking to the iron. Press with a moderately hot iron. After cooling, tear the backing paper from the fusible webbing and lay a piece of brightly coloured lamé over the adhesive (C). Press the layers with a moderately hot iron (again, using the parchment). This will form the background fabric. Apply another layer of fusible webbing (D). When cool, remove the backing paper and sprinkle on an assortment of cut up thread, tiny confetti-like bits of fabric, sequins, or bits of foil (E), without letting the bits overlap or they will not stick to the fabric. On top of these tiny bits, lay a piece of sheer fabric (F) to secure all the pieces, and provide added interest. Cover with a piece of greaseproof parchment and press with a moderately hot iron.

2 **Making shapes.** Select a shape from the templates. Using a photocopier, enlarge the shapes until the star measures 6in (15cm) from point to point. You could use any solid shape with this technique; biscuit cutters are ideal. You could make the shapes smaller or larger depending upon how you intend to use them. Once enlarged, trace the shapes on to the fabric and cut them out with scissors.

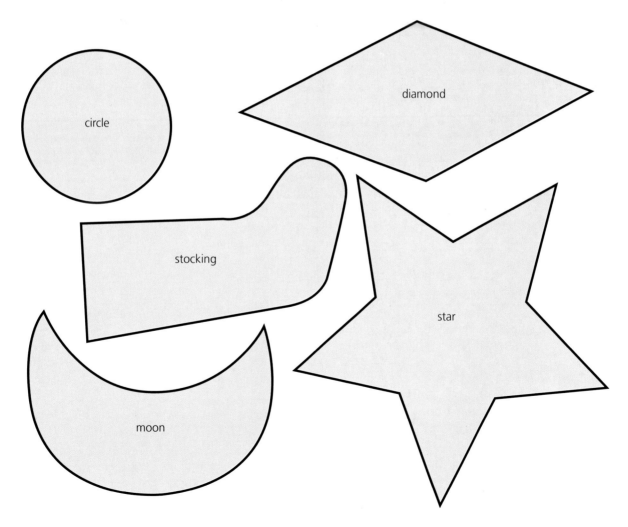

circle

diamond

stocking

star

moon

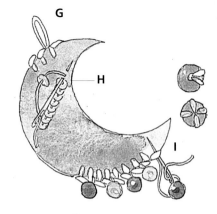

3 **Stitching options.** Add further interest with as much, or as little stitching as you want. Work directly into the edge of the shapes using overcast or buttonhole stitches. When working buttonhole stitch, let the looped part of the stitch lie directly along the edge of the fabric. This will help to create a sharp finish on the edge. Add extra beads, sequins or stars to the basic shape, or add them to the edges as the edge stitching is applied. Be sure to add a loop from which to hang or attach the decoration. Long looping dangles of threads, beads and sequins will add extra sparkle.

4 **Decorative stitches.** Make a loop (G) from which to hang the decoration while stitching the edge. Attach overlapping sequins using back stitch (H). Sequins provide glitter to the decoration. They can be also be attached using a straight holding stitch (I). For a raised effect, bring the needle up through the main bead or sequin, add another bead or sequin, and take the needle back down through the first. Beads can be added singly by merely passing a thread through the bead, attaching it to the decoration (J). Beads or sequins may be applied to the edge of the decoration using ordinary dressmaker's thread, and lacing between the edge stitches, adding beads or sequins as you go.

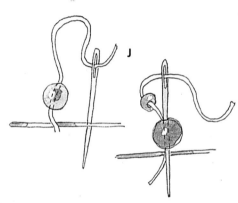

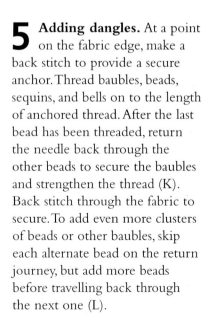

overcast edge

5 **Adding dangles.** At a point on the fabric edge, make a back stitch to provide a secure anchor. Thread baubles, beads, sequins, and bells on to the length of anchored thread. After the last bead has been threaded, return the needle back through the other beads to secure the baubles and strengthen the thread (K). Back stitch through the fabric to secure. To add even more clusters of beads or other baubles, skip each alternate bead on the return journey, but add more beads before travelling back through the next one (L).

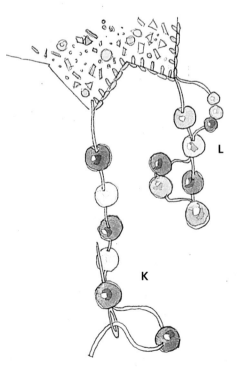

buttonhole stitch

THE CHRISTMAS STAR

There are few symbols more evocative of the story of Christmas than the star of the East that guided the shepherds and wise men to the manger of the Christ Child. 'Star of wonder, star of night…': make this decoration to adorn the tree, hang it from a light fitting, or use it to embellish a Christmas parcel.

YOU WILL NEED

- ☐ Christmassy pattern fabric that will suit a circular shape, 2 pieces 4 ¼in (11cm) diameter
- ☐ wadding 3in (7.7cm) diameter
- ☐ heavy cardboard 2 pieces 3in (7.7cm) diameter
- ☐ ribbon 1yd (1m) of ⅝in (15mm) wide. Cut 7 x 2 ½in (6.5cm) lengths
- ☐ ribbon 1yd (1m) of ⅛in (3mm) wide
- ☐ 7 bells or beads
- ☐ dressmaker's thread to match fabric
- ☐ large eye chenille needle
- ☐ glue
- ☐ scissors

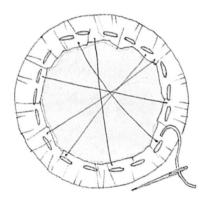

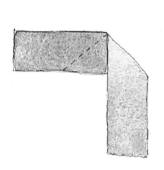

1 Making the star. Lightly glue the wadding to the cardboard circle.

2 Tack around the edge of the fabric circle leaving long tails on the thread. Place the wadded side of the card against the wrong side of the fabric. Gently pull the tails of the tacking thread until the fabric snugly encases the card. Thread the tails into a needle and lace across the back of the card (working stitches from one side to the other) to secure the fabric cover. Ensure that the gathers are evenly spaced around the back.

3 Prairie points. Lightly moisten the 2 ½in (6.5cm) lengths of ribbon. Fold them into points and press with an iron.

4 Stitch the prairie points into position evenly spaced around the back of the star.

5 **Ribbon loops.** Thread the ⅛in (3mm) ribbon through the needle. Leaving a small loop between each of the points (A), work around the back side of the circle by taking small running stitches between the points (B).

6 **Beading prairie points.** Fasten bells or beads securely to the points of the star by taking small stitches through the loop of the bells or through the eye of the beads (C). Sew on a hanging loop.

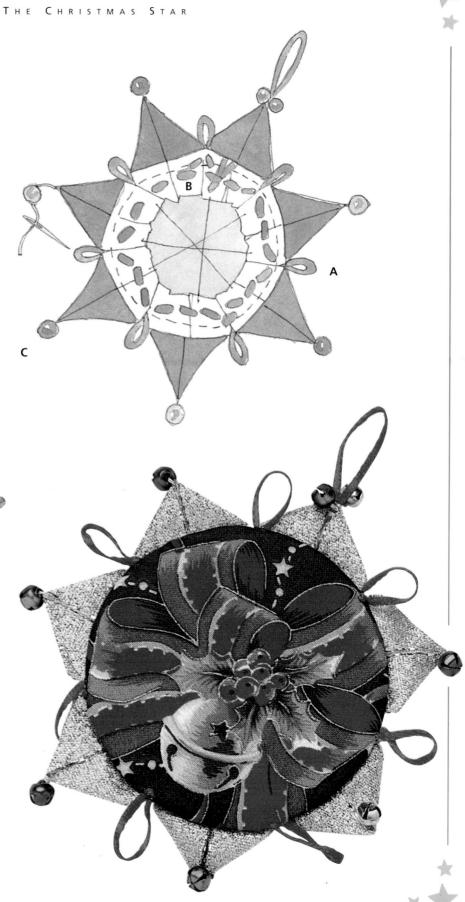

7 **Backing.** To make the star reversible, cut another piece of fabric and card the same as the front piece. Enclose the card as before. When completed, align the back and front and slip stitch them together. Alternatively, select a piece of fabric that will complement the star and fuse it directly to the back of the star with fusible webbing.

FABRIC ORIGAMI DECORATIONS

Fabric can be folded into wonderful three-dimensional origami decorations by applying a stiffening agent. Embellish the crisp folds and shapes with a few decorative stitches. Start with a paper model to test the pattern and save making folding errors and unnecessary creases in the fabric.

A

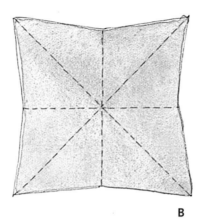

B

1 **The flute.** Stiffen the fabric before you start (refer to page 17 for instructions).
Fold the fabric in half across both diagonals, then turn it over (A). Then fold it in half on the horizontal and vertical (B). Collapse the folds to make a square (C).

2 Fold the top right-hand edge to the centre, mark the crease, then fold back (D).

3 Open the top right-hand layer (E). Flatten it across the square (F).

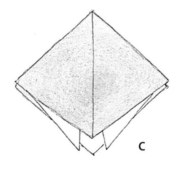

C

D

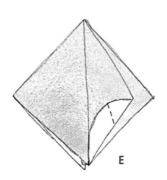

E

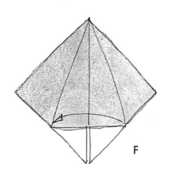

F

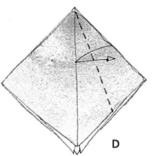

4 Fold over the top layer (G). Repeat steps 2 and 3 with the right-hand layer (D, E, F).

5 Fold over the top layer as before (H). Continue repeating steps 2 and 3 until the decoration is folded into a diamond shape (I, J).

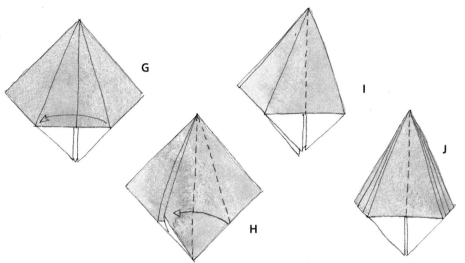

6 Make a second shape in the same way.

7 Slip the fluted pieces together, lapping the longer points under shorter points (K). Straighten the folds to finish.

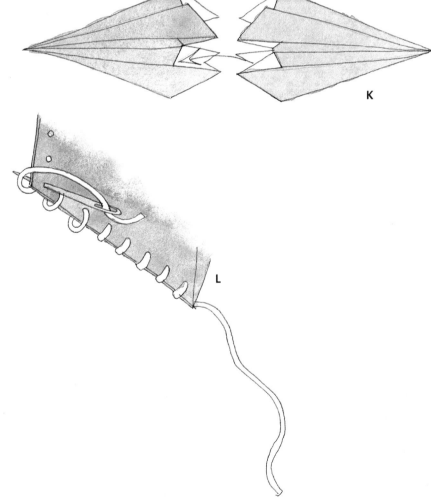

8 **Stitching the flute.** The stark lines of the flute may be embellished with the addition of decorative stitches. Thread the needle with the chosen ribbon. Insert the tip of the needle into one point of the decoration. Leave a tail of about 7in (18cm) trailing from the tip. Work stitches along an edge of the decoration through both layers of fabric along the creases using overcast stitch (L). When stitched, take the thread through the tip of the ornament leaving a tail of about 7in (18cm). Continue stitching along each crease of the flute, finishing off each time with a tail. Use the ribbon ends as decorative tassels at the top and bottom of the flute.

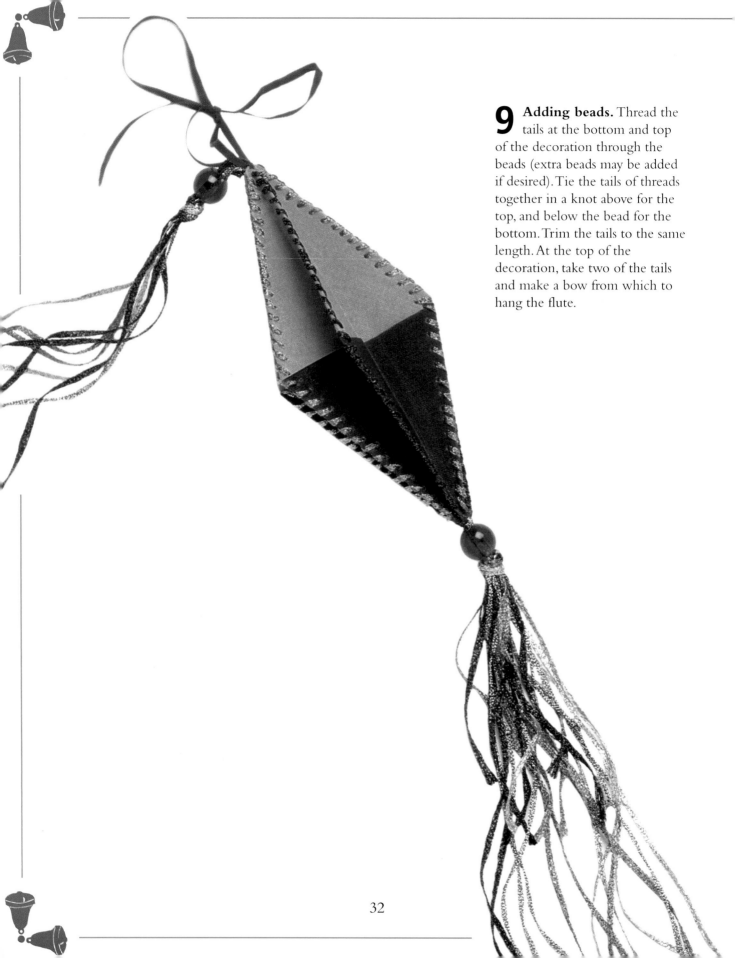

9 **Adding beads.** Thread the tails at the bottom and top of the decoration through the beads (extra beads may be added if desired). Tie the tails of threads together in a knot above for the top, and below the bead for the bottom. Trim the tails to the same length. At the top of the decoration, take two of the tails and make a bow from which to hang the flute.

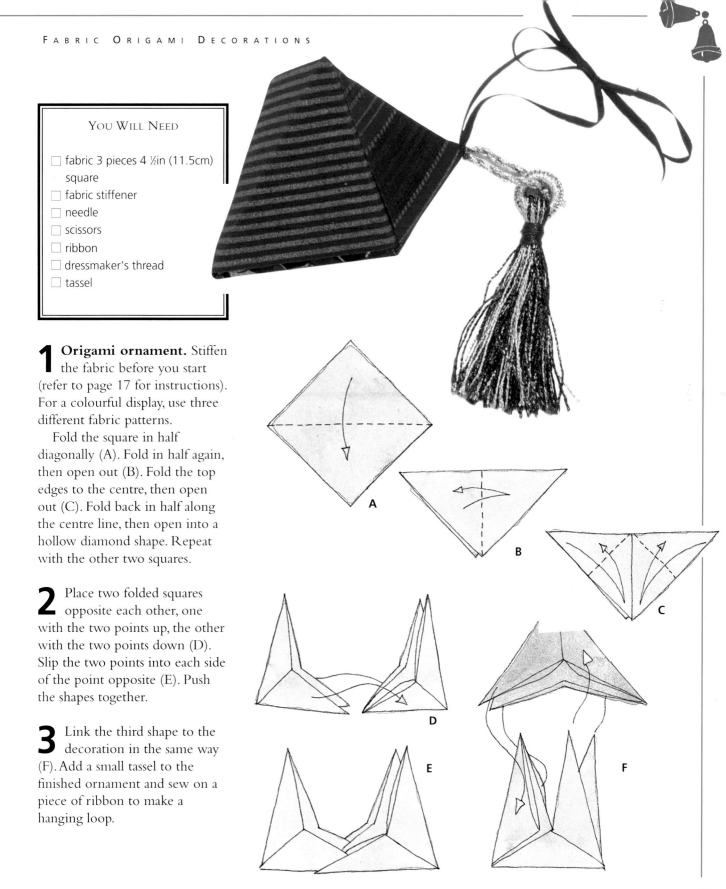

YOU WILL NEED

- [ ] fabric 3 pieces 4 ½in (11.5cm) square
- [ ] fabric stiffener
- [ ] needle
- [ ] scissors
- [ ] ribbon
- [ ] dressmaker's thread
- [ ] tassel

1 Origami ornament. Stiffen the fabric before you start (refer to page 17 for instructions). For a colourful display, use three different fabric patterns.

Fold the square in half diagonally (A). Fold in half again, then open out (B). Fold the top edges to the centre, then open out (C). Fold back in half along the centre line, then open into a hollow diamond shape. Repeat with the other two squares.

2 Place two folded squares opposite each other, one with the two points up, the other with the two points down (D). Slip the two points into each side of the point opposite (E). Push the shapes together.

3 Link the third shape to the decoration in the same way (F). Add a small tassel to the finished ornament and sew on a piece of ribbon to make a hanging loop.

A

B

C

D

E

F

1 **Christmas tree.** Stiffen the fabric before you start (refer to page 17 for instructions).

   Use several fabric squares graduated by ½in (1.25cm), or, if a larger tree is wanted, use fabrics graduated by 1in (2.5cm). This example uses three squares of fabric, but any number could be added. Make all the sizes of triangles in the same way, as shown in the artwork.

2 Fold each square in half diagonally (A). Fold in half again to make a guiding crease, then open out (B). Fold the top edges just beyond the guiding crease, making a triangular piece. Fasten with a spot of glue, alternating leaving right and left tips on the surface of each triangle to allow some variation in the segments (C).

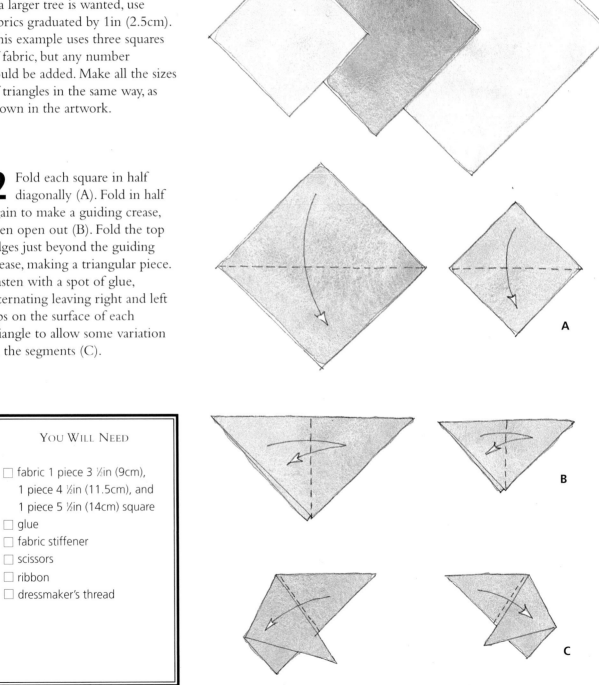

A

B

C

YOU WILL NEED

☐ fabric 1 piece 3 ½in (9cm), 1 piece 4 ½in (11.5cm), and 1 piece 5 ½in (14cm) square
☐ glue
☐ fabric stiffener
☐ scissors
☐ ribbon
☐ dressmaker's thread

3 Stack the segments by inserting a larger piece into a smaller one, and join them together with a spot of glue. Sew a ribbon on to the top to make a hanging loop.

BUTTONHOLE NAPKIN RINGS

These beautiful ornamental rings could be used as a gift, to embellish a cloth, or as part of a beautiful hanging tassel with a ring at the top of the tassel head. Larger rings could be embellished with stitches and used as napkins rings for special occasions. Look at the variations in the photograph on page 6.

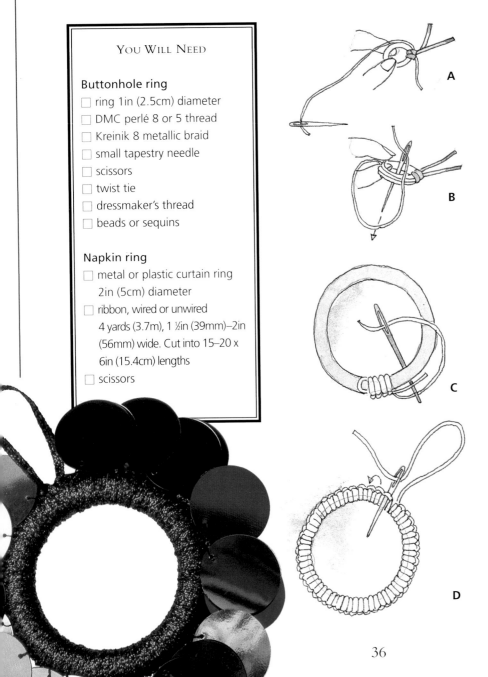

1 **Buttonhole ring.** Lay the thread around the outside edge of the ring, and temporarily secure it with a twist-tie (A).

2 Hold the ring in the left hand, and pinch the outside thread to the ring, a short distance from the twist-tie. Work buttonhole stitch over both the wrapped thread and the ring (B).

3 Work a few stitches until the thread wrapped around the ring is secure, then remove the twist-tie. Trim the tail of the thread close to the last stitch and continue buttonholing around the entire ring (C).

4 Make a loop from which to hang the ring, and secure the thread by working a few stitches through the first buttonhole loops (D).

5 You can add beads or sequins after the ring has been completed. Thread a small needle with a matching thread. Pick up beads or sequins one at a time on to the needle, and lace over and under the loops of the buttonhole stitches. Work as many around the edge as seems pleasing.

36

1 **Napkin ring.** You can singe
the cut ends of some ribbons
to achieve an unusual and
pleasing result. Singeing will stop
fraying. For safety's sake, the
singeing should be done with a
match at the kitchen sink, and
before attaching the ribbons on
the ring.

2 Tie each ribbon to the ring
using a reef knot. Continue
adding ribbons until the ring is
fat and crowded.

BUTTONS, BEADS AND SEQUINS

A brooch? A pendant? An embellishment for a present? A set of buttons? The imagination will dictate how these little jewel-like ornaments are made and used. Anything goes for these baubles. Pile on as many bright and sparkling bits, buttons, beads, sequins and pieces of fabric as pleases the eye.

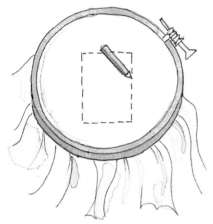

1 Stretch the fabric over an embroidery hoop or frame. Mark the outline of the decoration with a fabric pencil or an ordinary hard lead pencil. It could be a circle, triangle, oval, rectangle, diamond, square, or whatever takes your imagination. Cut a piece of stiff card the same size as the outline.

YOU WILL NEED

- ☐ sturdy fabric 2 x bigger than 3in (7.7cm) to 4in (10cm) square
- ☐ stiff card 2 x 3in (7.7cm) to 4in (10cm) square
- ☐ a selection of beads, buttons, bells and sequins
- ☐ buttonhole rings
- ☐ small Christmas decorations
- ☐ twisted cords
- ☐ needles
- ☐ dressmaker's thread
- ☐ embroidery hoop or frame
- ☐ hard lead pencil
- ☐ scissors

2 Sew on the larger objects. The biggest bits should be kept around the bottom edge of the outline; mount rings on their side to develop height; wrap cords through and around buttonhole rings. A cord could be couched on to the fabric to add a more structured look. Do not stitch over the edge of the outline, but let the bits droop over the edges of the shape to create a soft look.

3 Remove the embroidery from the frame. Cut away the background fabric leaving a 1in (2.5cm) border around the drawn outline. Run a tacking stitch around the edge of the cut shape. Lay the piece of card on the wrong side of the fabric and taking stitches alternately from each side of the embroidery, lace the embroidery tautly over the card. Sew on a hanging loop. Follow step 7 for finishing the Christmas star (page 29).

DECORATIVE CORDS

*If you cannot find exactly the cord you want in the shops, make one yourself.
As ornate, complex, and beautiful, as some of these cords may be, they are
deceptively simple to make. Use them as garlands to decorate the Christmas tree,
straps for purses and bags, or embellishments for any number of decorations.*

1 Decide how long you want the finished cord to be and start with a bundle of threads six times that length. As you work the cord it will shrink in size. Take the bundle of threads, fold them in half and tie a knot in one end.

2 Loop them over a hook. Using a pencil stuck in the end of the thread bundle or a hand drill fitted with a large cup hook as a twisting mechanism, stretch the strands out to full length (A). Twist the cord, keeping it under sufficient tension that it does not knot up while twisting. When knots seem to form regardless of tension, the cord is sufficiently twisted (B).

3 Keeping the cord under tension, remove it from the twister. Fold it in half, and lift the end from the twister on to the hook (C). Maintain the tension at all times. Release the cord where it has been held at the mid point. As it wraps itself into a single strand, use your hands to smooth out any bumps that may form. Remove the cord from the hook and wrap a twist-tie around the ends to hold the cord and prevent it unravelling until it is finished.

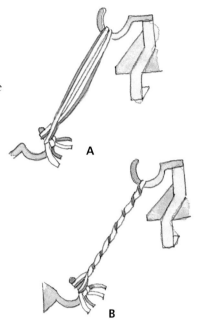

A

B

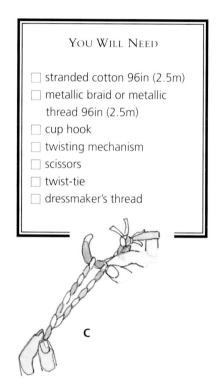

C

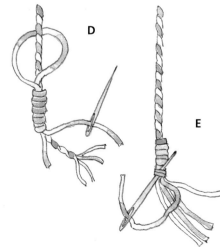

D

E

YOU WILL NEED

- ☐ stranded cotton 96in (2.5m)
- ☐ metallic braid or metallic thread 96in (2.5m)
- ☐ cup hook
- ☐ twisting mechanism
- ☐ scissors
- ☐ twist-tie
- ☐ dressmaker's thread

4 **Fringe on the cord end.** Using a co-ordinating colour, lay a loop of thread alongside the cord. Wrap it around several times, working towards the short end of the thread near to the end of the cord (D). Pull the short end of the loop thread to create a smooth finished edge.

5 Take the needle through the last few wraps to secure the end of the thread (E). Trim it and unravel the cord up to the bottom of the wrapping.

40

TEDDY BEAR STOCKING

The miniature Christmas stocking, with its teddy bear design, is a lovely, decoration, which you can hang on a tree, or use in some other festive way. It's a super project which combines a variety of threads and textures to create a Christmas treat which will be enjoyed by the whole family for years to come.

1 Hat. Fill in hat area with diagonal tent stitch, using two strands of medici wool 8127 red. A small area of shading will require DMC medici wool 8126 dark red.

2 Hat border and pompom (made to look like fur). Outline in French knots using medici wool 7380 grey. Fill in using medici wool white, using French knots. There will be a large quantity of French knots.

3 Body. Outline the body in horizontal tent stitch using medici wool 8324 gold. To fill in the body, use two strands of medici wool 8502 light brown, working in split stitch.

4 Scarf. Work horizontal stitch with medici wool 8127 red, stranded cotton 909 green, stranded cotton 310 black. Use two strands of each of these colours.

5 Holly. Work diagonal tent stitch using stranded cotton 909 green. Work the berries in French knots with five strands of stranded cotton 310 black.

YOU WILL NEED

- [ ] 18 gauge, Zweigart mono canvas 8in (20cm) square
- [ ] DMC medici wool 8127 red
- [ ] DMC medici wool 8126 dark red
- [ ] DMC medici wool 7380 light grey
- [ ] DMC medici wool white
- [ ] DMC medici wool 8324 gold
- [ ] DMC medici wool 8502 light brown
- [ ] DMC stranded cotton 909 green
- [ ] DMC stranded cotton 310 black
- [ ] DMC stranded cotton 498 red
- [ ] Kreinik 16 metallic braid 032 white
- [ ] DMC medici wool ecru

- [ ] DMC perlé 5 green
- [ ] green or red velvet
- [ ] lining fabric
- [ ] tapestry needle
- [ ] dressmaker's thread
- [ ] embroidery hoop or frame
- [ ] paper
- [ ] twisted cord
- [ ] scissors

Stitch chart
1 square = 1 stitch

Stitches. Tent stitch, diagonal tent stitch, French knots, mosaic stitch, split stitch (pages 18–19).

6 Eyes and nose. Fill in with French knots worked in stranded cotton 310 black. Wrap the thread one turn around the needle for the eyes. Make two wraps of thread around the needle for the French knots on the nose.

7 Stocking border. Work three rows of mosaic stitch. Work the top row in stranded cotton 498 red. Work the second row in stranded cotton 909 green. The third row is worked using stranded cotton 498 red. Two rows of the chart represent one row of mosaic stitch in one colour.

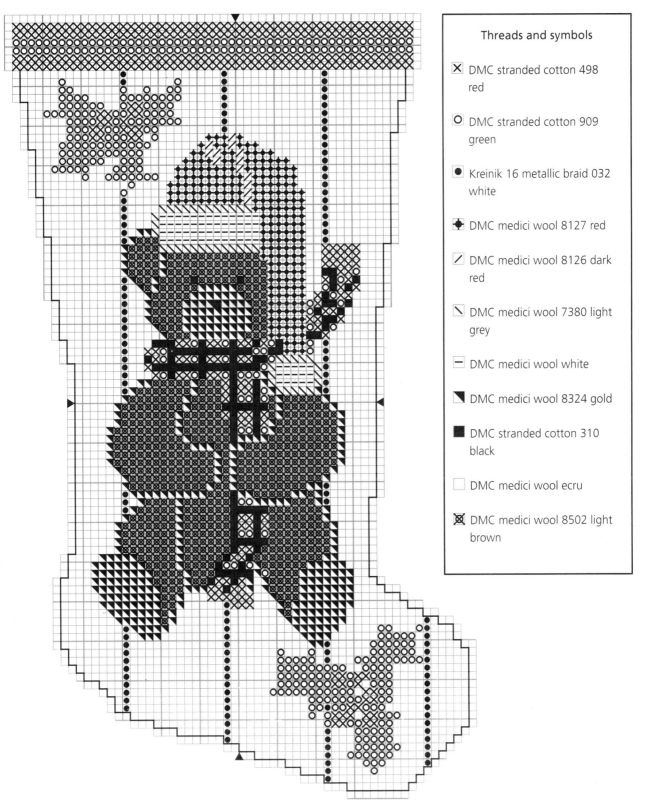

Threads and symbols

☒ DMC stranded cotton 498 red

⊙ DMC stranded cotton 909 green

● Kreinik 16 metallic braid 032 white

◆ DMC medici wool 8127 red

╱ DMC medici wool 8126 dark red

╲ DMC medici wool 7380 light grey

— DMC medici wool white

◣ DMC medici wool 8324 gold

■ DMC stranded cotton 310 black

☐ DMC medici wool ecru

⊠ DMC medici wool 8502 light brown

8 Background. Note the four vertical lines that run the length of the stocking. Work the lines in Kreinik 16 metallic braid 032 white, using horizontal tent stitch. Use tent stitch to fill in the remainder of the stocking shape, using two strands of medici wool ecru. When finished, carefully cut around the stocking leaving a seam allowance of ⅝in (1.6cm).

9 Backing. Lay the cut out stocking on a piece of paper and trace around its edge. Cut a paper pattern the same size as the stocking. Cut a piece of green or red velvet using the paper pattern. Lay the velvet, right side down, on the front of the stocking. Stitch around

the edge using either hand or machine stitches. Leave the stocking open across the top edge. When finished, trim the seams and turn the stocking to the right side.

10 Lining. Using the paper stocking pattern, cut two matching pieces of fabric. Stitch these together, right sides facing, leaving the top open, and trim the seams. Insert the lining into the stocking, gently working it down into the toe. Round the top, turn the canvas and velvet lining edges over to meet each other, and stitch a neat overcast stitch around the top edge to securely fix the lining to the stocking.

11 Twisted cord. Either buy or make a 30in (77cm) green twisted cord to stitch around the edge of the stocking. To make a twisted cord use DMC perlé 5 green. Hand stitch the cord around the edge of the stocking, leaving a small loop from which to hang it.

NINE DRUMMERS DRUMMING

From the traditional Christmas song, The Twelve Days of Christmas, come nine drummers drumming. Marching in rank and file, these colourful little characters will add instant drama when they're hung from your festive tree or around your home. This circular canvas work is 4in (10cm) in diameter.

1 Bearskin hat. Tent stitch in two strands of medici wool black.

2 Boots. Tent stitch Kreinik 16 metallic braid 005 black.

3 Uniform. Tent stitch the uniform in two strands of medici wool 8666 red.

4 Background. Vertical tent stitch, alternating between Rainbow gallery neon rays 02 silver, 92 white, and Kreinik 16 metallic braid 032 white.

5 Uniform. Start with one drummer and work the shading in tent stitch, adding gold on drums, drumsticks and hands. Shade between legs and arms using two strands of medici wool 8102 dark red. Use Kreinik 16 metallic braid 002 gold for the epaulettes.

6 Drums and drumsticks. Tent stitch drums in five strands of stranded cotton 699 green. Highlights are worked in Kreinik 16 metallic braid 002 gold. Work drumsticks in five strands of stranded cotton 434 brown.

YOU WILL NEED

- [ ] 18 gauge, Zweigart mono canvas 8in (20cm) square
- [ ] DMC medici wool black
- [ ] Kreinik 16 metallic braid 005 black
- [ ] DMC medici wool 8666 red
- [ ] Rainbow gallery neon rays 02 silver and 92 grey white
- [ ] Kreinik 16 metallic braid 032 white
- [ ] DMC medici wool 8102 dark red
- [ ] Kreinik 16 metallic braid 002 gold
- [ ] DMC stranded cotton 699 green
- [ ] Kreinik 8 metallic braid 002 gold
- [ ] DMC stranded cotton 434 brown
- [ ] DMC stranded cotton 754 pink
- [ ] DMC fil or clair gold metallic
- [ ] DMC stranded cotton 310 black
- [ ] velvet 4in (10cm) circle plus ⅝in (1.6cm) seam allowance
- [ ] polyester or toy stuffing
- [ ] tapestry needles 22, 24
- [ ] dressmaker's thread
- [ ] embroidery hoop or frame
- [ ] twisted cord 20in (51cm)
- [ ] scissors

Stitch Chart
1 square = 1 stitch

Stitches. Tent stitch, cross stitch, overstitching (pages 18-20).

---

7 Hair. Work the hair using five strands of stranded cotton 434 brown.

8 Hands and faces. Use five strands of stranded cotton 754 pink, or choose your own suitable colour.

9 Bearskin tassels. Make nine miniature tassels approximately ⅜in (1cm) long. Make the tassels using Kreinik 8 metallic braid 002 gold. Stitch tassels to hats about ¾in (2cm) to ⅞in (2.3cm) down the hat.

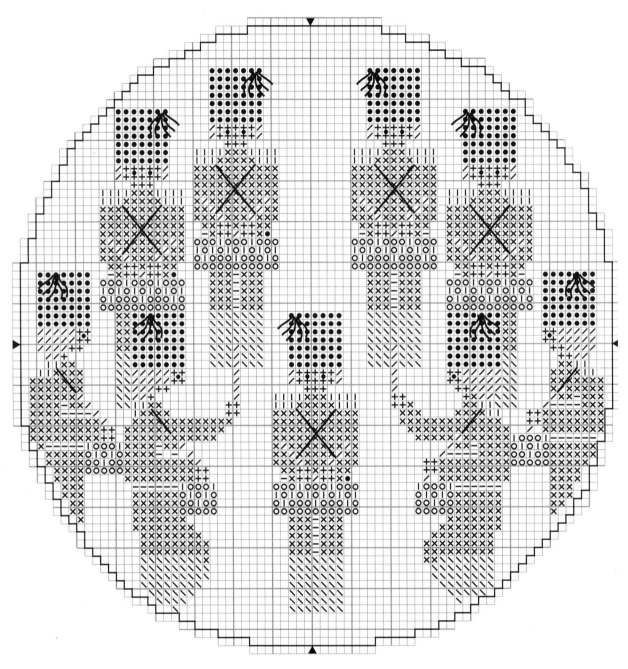

Thread and symbols chart

● DMC medici wool black	− DMC medici wool 8102 dark red	**Overstitching**
╱ DMC stranded cotton 434 brown	╲ Kreinik 16 metallic braid 005 black	Work cross on uniform in single strand
+ DMC stranded cotton 754 pink	☐ Neon rays 02 silver	of Kreinik metallic braid gold
O DMC stranded cotton 699 green	Neon rays 92 grey-white	DMC stranded cotton black for eyes
✕ DMC medici wool 8666 red	Kreinik 16 metallic braid 032 white	Kreinik 16 metallic braid 002 gold
I Kreinik 16 metallic braid 002 gold		tassels on bearskins

10 **Crossing belts.** Use fil or clair metallic thread to make cross stitches where they are indicated.

11 **Eyes.** After the face has been stitched, use three strands of stranded cotton 310 black. Locate eye position and catch a small amount of the previously worked stitch. Take the needle back through the same hole as the previous stitch, and secure the thread to the back of the canvas. Eyes are pinpoint size.

12 **Finishing.** After all stitching has been completed, carefully cut the decoration from the canvas leaving a ⅝in (1.6cm) seam allowance of empty canvas around the edges of the design.

13 Lay velvet lining fabric against the decoration, right sides together. Place pins around the edge and tack the two layers together, working from the canvas side. Stitch the seam by hand or machine using a strong, matching dressmaker's thread. Leave an open space of about 2in (5cm) for you to turn the decoration. Cut notches in the seam allowance around the edge to reduce bulk. Pull the decoration inside out, through the hole, and firmly stuff the inside. Stitch the opening together using small slip stitches, leaving a small space for inserting the cords.

14 **Cord and hanging loop.** Either make a cord, or buy one to apply to the edge of the decoration. Begin applying the cord at the centre point between the hats of the two topmost drummers. Tuck the ends of cord into space previously left open. Slip stitch the cord around the decoration, by hand. When the starting point is reached, make a loop with the cord from which to hang the decoration, then secure the end.

TEN PIPERS PIPING

To accompany the nine drummers, there are ten pipers piping to make the Christmas group complete. Make a combination of the two and bring a Christmas classic song to life. The finished size of this decoration is about 4in (10cm) in diameter.

1 **Jacket and caps for pipers 1, 3, 6, 8, and 10.** Work tent stitch with two strands of medici wool 8666 red.

2 **Borders on all caps and socks.** Work tent stitch with five strands of stranded cotton white.

3 **Faces, knees and hands.** Work tent stitch with five strands of stranded cotton 754 pink.

YOU WILL NEED

- ☐ 18 gauge, Zweigart mono canvas 8in (20cm) square
- ☐ DMC medici wool 8666 red
- ☐ DMC stranded cotton white
- ☐ DMC stranded cotton 754 pink
- ☐ DMC medici wool 8508 dark grey
- ☐ DMC medici wool 8102 dark red
- ☐ DMC stranded cotton 310 black
- ☐ Kreinik 16 metallic braid 002 gold
- ☐ DMC medici wool 8839 brown
- ☐ Rainbow gallery neon rays 32 shiny green
- ☐ DMC stranded cotton 798 blue
- ☐ Rainbow gallery neon rays 20 shiny red

- ☐ DMC medici wool 8415 green
- ☐ velvet 4in (10cm) circle plus ⅝in (1.6cm) seam allowance
- ☐ polyester or toy stuffing
- ☐ tapestry needles 22, 24
- ☐ dressmaker's thread
- ☐ embroidery hoop or frame
- ☐ twisted cord 20in (51cm)
- ☐ scissors

Stitch chart
1 square = 1 stitch

Stitches. Tent stitch, overstitching (refer to page 18–20 for stitch instructions).

---

4 **Hair and beards.** Work tent stitch with two strands of medici wool 8508 dark grey.

5 **Shading on arms of pipers 1, 3, 6, 8, and 10.** Work tent stitch with two strands of medici wool 8102 dark red.

6 **Arms of pipers 2, 4, 5, 7, and 9.** Work tent stitch with five strands of stranded cotton 310 black.

7 **Horns.** Work tent stitch in Kreinik 16 metallic braid 002 gold.

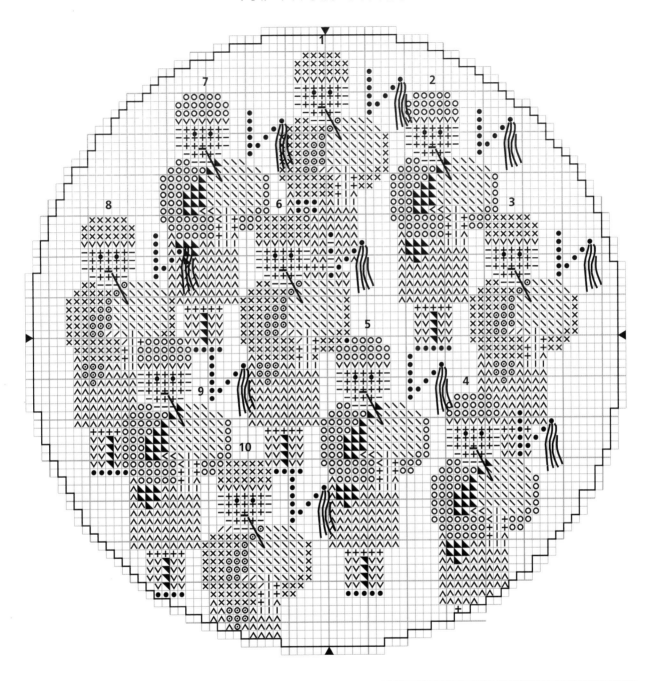

Thread and symbols chart

☒ DMC medici wool 8666 red	⊙ Neon rays 32 green	**Overstitching**
☒ DMC stranded cotton white	◣ DMC stranded cotton 798	DMC stranded cotton black for eyes
✚ DMC stranded cotton 754 pink	● DMC 310 black	Straight stitch from bag to mouth
— DMC medici wool 8508 dark grey	◤ Neon rays 20 red	Red and green tassels
╱ DMC medici wool 8102 dark red	◯ DMC medici wool 8415 green	
˂ DMC stranded cotton 310 black	⋀ DMC medici wool 8415, 8666	
❙ Kreinik 16 metallic braid 002 gold	one strand of each mixed	
╲ DMC medici wool 8839 brown		

8 **Bags.** Work tent stitch with two strands of medici wool 8839 brown

9 **Sash on pipers 1, 3, 6, 8, and 10.** Work tent stitch in Rainbow gallery neon rays 32 shiny green.

10 **Shading between legs and background.** Work tent stitch with two strands of stranded cotton 798 blue.

11 **Pipes and shoes.** Work tent stitch with five strands of stranded cotton 310 black

12 **Pipers 2, 4, 5, 7, and 9.** Work tent stitch for the sash in neon rays 20 shiny red.

13 **Jackets and caps on pipers 2, 4, 5, 7, and 9.** Work tent stitch with two strands of medici wool 8415 green.

14 **Kilts.** Work tent stitch in medici wool 8666 red and 8415 green. Use one strand of each colour to create tartan effect on kilts.

15 **Eyes and mouths.** After all canvas work has been worked, use three strands of stranded cotton 310 black and bring the needle up from the back of the canvas at the correct point for the eyes. Catch a small amount of the surface stitch, and take the needle back down through the same hole. Eyes are pinpoint size.

16 **Pipes.** Use five strands of stranded cotton 310 black to make one long stitch from piper's mouth to the bag. The other two pipes have already been worked in tent stitch. Work each of the remaining pipers in the same way.

17 **Tassels.** Use three strands each of medici wool 8415 green and 8666 red to make ten tassels. One end of each tassel is stitched to the top of each piper's pipe so it will hang free from the surface of the canvas.

18 **Finishing.** After all stitching has been completed, carefully cut the decoration from the canvas, leaving a ⅝in (1.6cm) seam allowance of empty canvas around the edges of the design.

19 Lay the velvet lining fabric against the decoration, right sides together. Place pins around the edge and tack the two layers together, working from the canvas side. Stitch the seam by hand or machine using a strong, matching dressmaker's thread. Leave an open space of about 2in (5cm) to turn the decoration. Cut notches in the seam allowance around the edge to reduce bulk. Pull the decoration inside out, through the hole, and firmly stuff the inside with wadding. Stitch the opening together using small slip stitches, leaving a small space for inserting the cords.

20 **Cord and hanging loop.** Either make a cord, or buy one to apply to the edge of the decoration. Start the cord at the tallest piper. Tuck the ends of cord into the space previously left open. Slip stitch the cord around the decoration by hand. When the starting point is reached, make a loop with the cord from which to hang the decoration, then secure the end.

FABRIC ORIGAMI GIFT BAGS

When fabric is properly prepared, it can be folded, using traditional origami concepts, into decorative bags suitable for any occasion. These bags are much stronger than paper ones and can be decorated using all kinds of conventional needlework techniques.

1 Work out how big the bag should be in order to contain the gift. Cut a fabric of your choice into a piece that is three times the height and twice the width of the item. Stiffen the fabric before you start (refer to page 17 for instructions).

2 Make a light crease to mark the centre at the top and bottom. Fold down in half, then open (A). Fold the edges towards the centre (B). Fold the edges to the outside edge (C). Then fold the fabric in half with the folds on the outside (D).

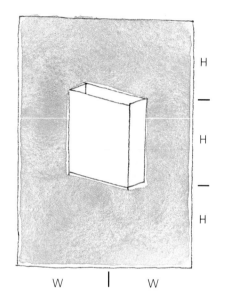

H

H

H

W | W

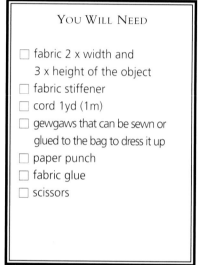

YOU WILL NEED

☐ fabric 2 x width and
   3 x height of the object
☐ fabric stiffener
☐ cord 1yd (1m)
☐ gewgaws that can be sewn or
   glued to the bag to dress it up
☐ paper punch
☐ fabric glue
☐ scissors

A	B	C	D

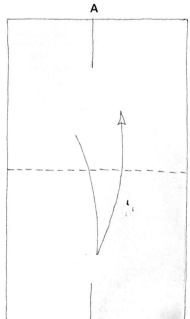

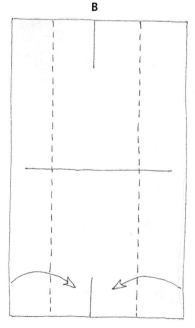

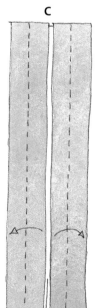

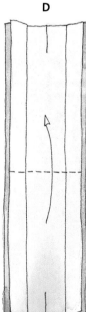

3 Fold down the corners (E). Make a crease by folding the top layer upwards (F). Open the corners. Turn over and repeat the last 2 steps. Open out the fabric but keep it folded just in half.

4 Fold the top hem upwards and crease the top fold (G). Turn over and fold up the second hem (H).

E

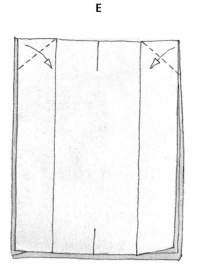

F

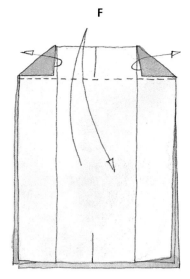

G

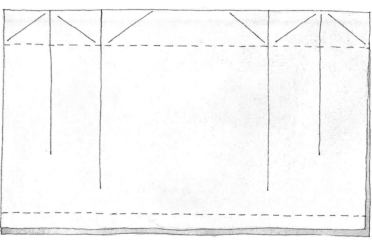

H

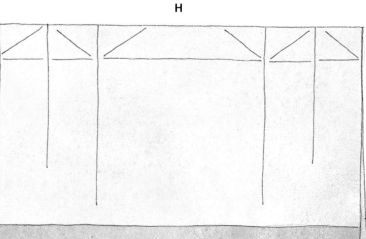

FABRICS

If you are unsure about which fabric to use, choose 100% cotton fabric. It retains the crisp folds that contribute to clear design lines. Try an attractive Christmas pattern. Other natural fabrics like silk and fine wool also produce interesting effects.

5 Fully open out the fabric (I). Fold the edges toward the centre (J).

6 Folding on the diagonal and the top of the central square of fold lines, fold up one side of the bag (K). Repeat with the other side (L), making two triangles at the base (M).

7 Glue the sides together. Lift and refold the hems together. You will now have a finished bag (N).

8 Punch holes in the top of the bag and thread through the cord to make a handle. Decorate with ribbons or other embellishments.

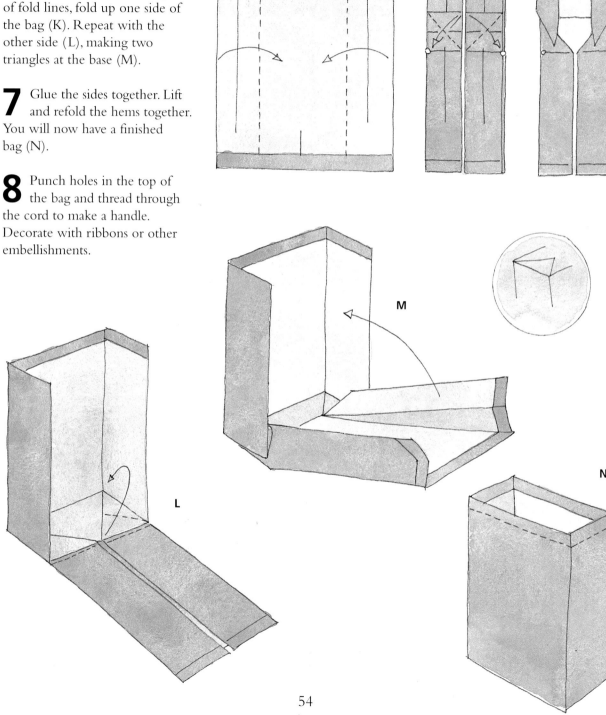

MINIATURE GIFT BAGS

Precious little bags, small enough to fit in the palm of your hand, each one is unique and will tell its recipient how much they are loved. They could be used to hold rings, tiny gifts, or exotic spices for your favourite cook. Make twenty-five and give them as daily advent gifts.

YOU WILL NEED

- [ ] fabric 6in (15cm) x 12in (31cm)
- [ ] fabric for fringe
- [ ] lining fabric 6in (15cm) x 12in (31cm)
- [ ] thin cord 2 x 24in (62cm)
- [ ] twisted cord
- [ ] template card 4 ¼in (10.9cm) x 5 ¼in (13.4cm)
- [ ] needle
- [ ] dressmaker's thread
- [ ] marker pen

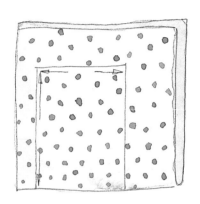

1 Fold the bag fabric in half and place the template with its short edge, 4 ¼in (10.9cm), on the fold of the fabric, at a pleasing part of the fabric design. Trace a light line around the template and cut the fabric. Do the same for the lining.

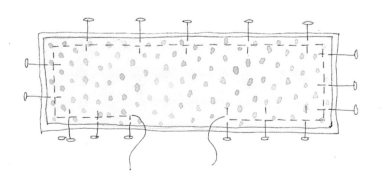

2 With right sides facing, pin together the bag fabric and lining fabric. Stitch the fabric together leaving a seam allowance of ⅝in (1.6cm). On a long side, leave a 2in (5cm) gap through which to turn the fabric.

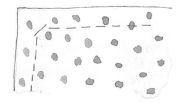

3 As you stitch towards the corners, take a diagonal stitch across the corner.

4 Trim excess fabric from around the seam to reduce bulk. Turn the fabric inside out and press the seams. Work a straight stitch close to the edges. Stitch the gap closed using small slip stitches.

5 Lay the fabric out and fold under a strip, ⅞in (2.3cm) wide at one end. Press the fold and stitch in place. Stitch another line ⅝in (1.6cm) in, from the outer edge. Do the same on the other end of the fabric. These are the channels for the cords.

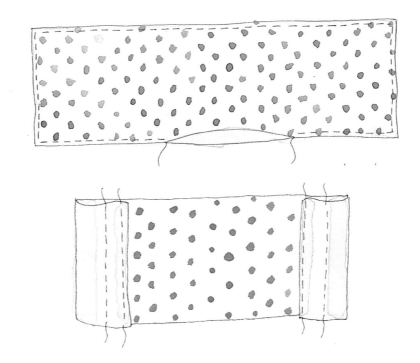

6 Fold the bag in half, bringing the cord channels together at the top. Stitch each side of the bag together, starting below the cord channel.

7 Using a bodkin or large tapestry needle, thread one of the cords, from the right, through the front and back channel. Thread the other cord, from the left, also through the front and back channel. The cords will run in opposite directions.

8 Tie the cords together in pairs to prevent the cords coming out of the channels. Sew on sequins, beads, or other decorations.

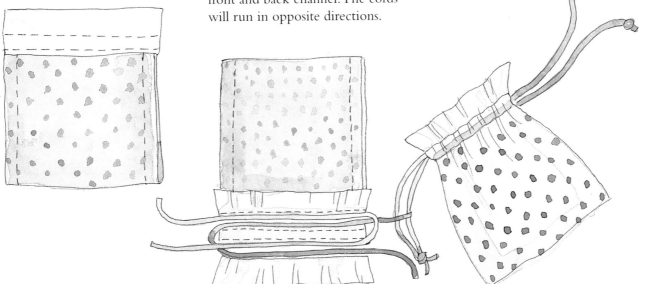

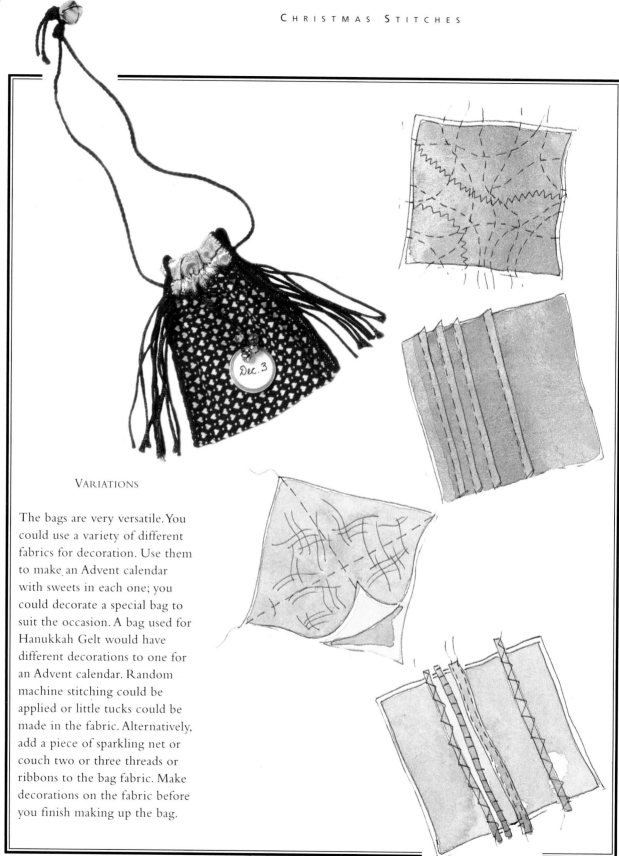

VARIATIONS

The bags are very versatile. You could use a variety of different fabrics for decoration. Use them to make an Advent calendar with sweets in each one; you could decorate a special bag to suit the occasion. A bag used for Hanukkah Gelt would have different decorations to one for an Advent calendar. Random machine stitching could be applied or little tucks could be made in the fabric. Alternatively, add a piece of sparkling net or couch two or three threads or ribbons to the bag fabric. Make decorations on the fabric before you finish making up the bag.

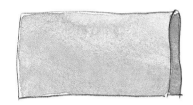

1 **Adding fringes.** Fringes can add a whole new dimension to the appearance of the little bags. Cut strips from the same fabric as the bag or a complementary material. Fold over a piece of fabric and cut it to the size of the bag.

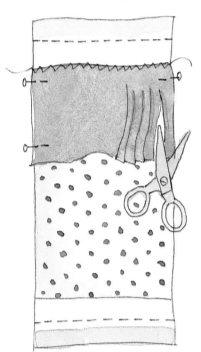

2 Lay the fabric with the fold against the cord channel. Stitch the top edge of the fold to the bag using a narrow zig-zag stitch. Before sewing the sides of the bag together, cut this fabric into vertical strips about ¼in (0.5cm) wide.

3 Fringe may be cut and arranged in any number of ways on the bag.

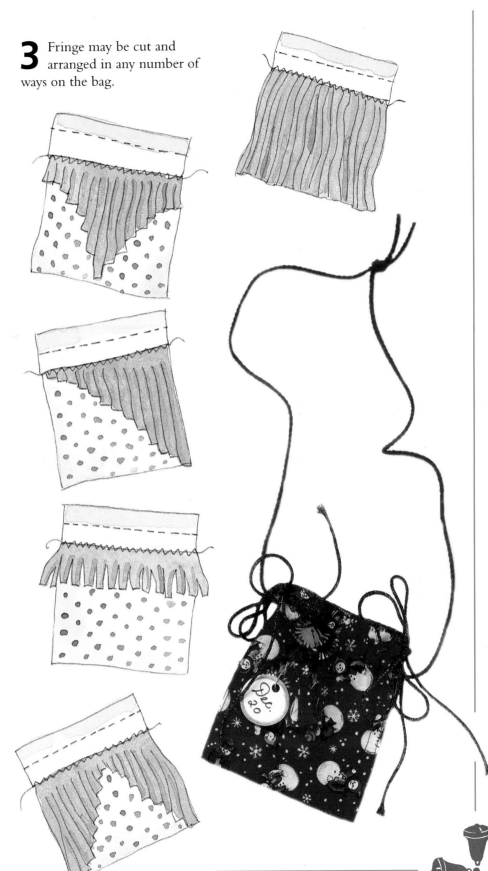

1 **Decorative cords, ribbons and threads.** Add these elements to the bag as it is being made. Follow the instructions to step 4. Then stitch a twisted cord or heavy thread to the edges of the fabric before moving on to the next step. The cords and threads could hang loosely, be tied into bows, or made into tassels.

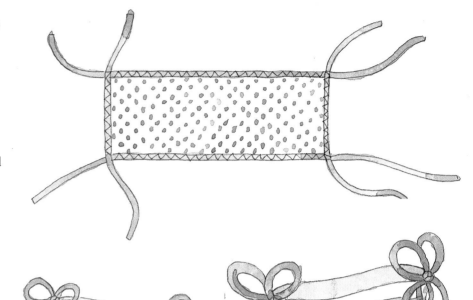

2 To tie bows at each side, thread a bead on to the cord and position it at the bottom edge. Tie a knot in the cord to secure the bead.

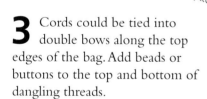

3 Cords could be tied into double bows along the top edges of the bag. Add beads or buttons to the top and bottom of dangling threads.

4 Tie knots to hold beads in position. Thread a bead on to each ribbon or cord at the top edge of the bag. Eight beads will be needed. Tie a knot to secure the beads.

POINSETTIA BOOK COVERS

Found in the desolation of the western American desert, the poinsettia displays its wonderful crown of bright red leaves at Christmas time. Bring this beautiful wild desert plant into your home as a book cover dedicated to a special person. The size of the book covers can be adjusted to suit any book.

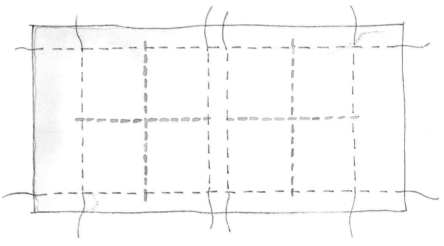

YOU WILL NEED

- [ ] square book 7 ¼in (18.6 cm) x 7 ¼in (18.6 cm) x ¾in (2cm)
- [ ] 20 gauge, Zweigart or Valerie mono canvas 10 ½in (26.5cm) x 19in (49.5cm), mushroom
- [ ] DMC stranded cotton yellow or gold
- [ ] DMC 3 perlé green
- [ ] DMC 5 perlé red
- [ ] tapestry needle 20/120
- [ ] dressmaker's thread
- [ ] embroidery hoop or frame

Stitch chart

1 square = 2 fabric threads

Stitches. Satin stitch, French knots, straight stitch, running stitch, buttonhole stitch, detached chain stitch, hem stitch (pages 20-21).

1 Red poinsettia cover.
Prepare the fabric before working any stitches. Referring to the diagram above, tack lines to mark out front, back, and all areas that are turned. Count threads horizontally and vertically to find the exact centre of both front and back panels. Mark the centres of each of the panels with tacking threads.

2 Work your embroidery following the chart. Each square represents two fabric threads. The corners indicate two small red buds worked in eight straight stitches coming from the same hole. These are worked in DMC 5 perlé red. The surrounding satin stitch leaves are worked in DMC 3 perlé green. The satin stitch border worked in DMC 3 perlé green makes a frame line surrounding the poinsettia. The back cover border is worked in the same colours and threads as the front.

3 The poinsettia leaves are worked in the centre of the front cover. In the middle of the leaves, are yellow or gold flowers stitched in French knots using six strands of stranded cotton. The red leaves surrounding the yellow flowers are worked in satin stitch using DMC 5 perlé red. The green leaves surrounding the red are worked in satin stitch using DMC 3 perlé green.

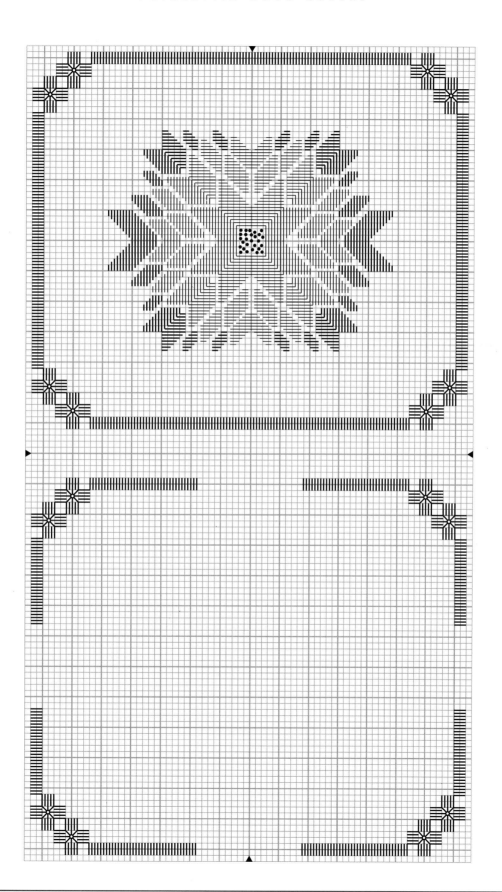

4 **Hem stitching fabric edges.** If you prefer, you could work hem stitch over the right and left hand edges as a more decorative alternative to a line of zig-zag or straight stitch. These edges will be seen on the inside front and back covers. Withdraw a thread from the fabric about ½in (1.25cm) from the edge.

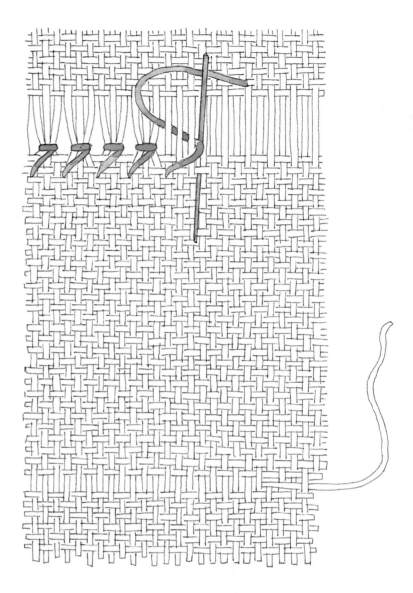

5 Working from left to right, using three strands of a matching colour of stranded cotton or DMC 12 perlé, hem stitch across the space created by the withdrawn thread. Begin at the bottom left. Take the thread across the front of the fabric. Wrap the hem stitch thread around two or three weft threads of the fabric. Take the needle to the start position for the next stitch, at the front of the fabric. Continue working in this fashion across the fabric. At the end of the row, secure the thread by weaving it in and out of the fabric a few times.

6 **Decorative fringe.** Withdraw any remaining threads below the hem stitch. Trim the weft to make a neat even line of fringe. This technique creates a nice finished edge without the bulk of a turned edge.

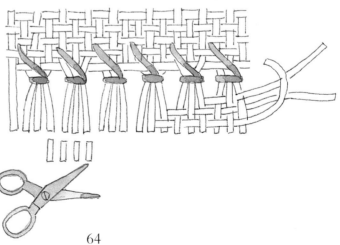

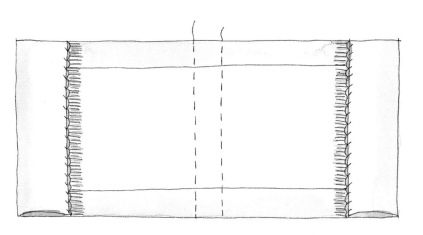

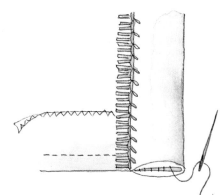

7 **Construction.** After completing all stitching, follow the tacking lines and fold the edges under, to the wrong side. Pin the edges in place and check the cover fits the book.

8 Make any necessary adjustments and stitch the front and back folds together. Using a matching dressmaker's thread, make inconspicuous running stitches to secure the top and bottom folds. Use small slip stitches to close the bottom and top of the right and left hand edges.

1 **Long red poinsettia book cover.** This photograph shows the back of the book cover. You can see the front on page 73.

2 Prepare the fabric following the instructions for the poinsettia book cover (page 62). Use the measurements below.

3 Work the embroidery following the chart on page 67. Stitches are the same as those used in the previous book cover. Detached chain stitch is used at opposite ends of the flower.

4 To finish the book cover, follow steps 4 to 8 of the preceeding book cover.

YOU WILL NEED

☐ long book 9 ¼in (23.5cm) x 4 ¾in (12cm) x 1in (2.5cm)
☐ 20 gauge, Zweigart Valerie mono canvas 12 ½in (33.5cm) x 14in (36cm), mushroom
☐ DMC stranded cotton yellow or gold
☐ DMC 3 perlé green
☐ DMC 5 perlé red
☐ tapestry needle 20
☐ dressmaker's thread
☐ embroidery hoop or frame

Stitch chart
1 square = 2 fabric threads

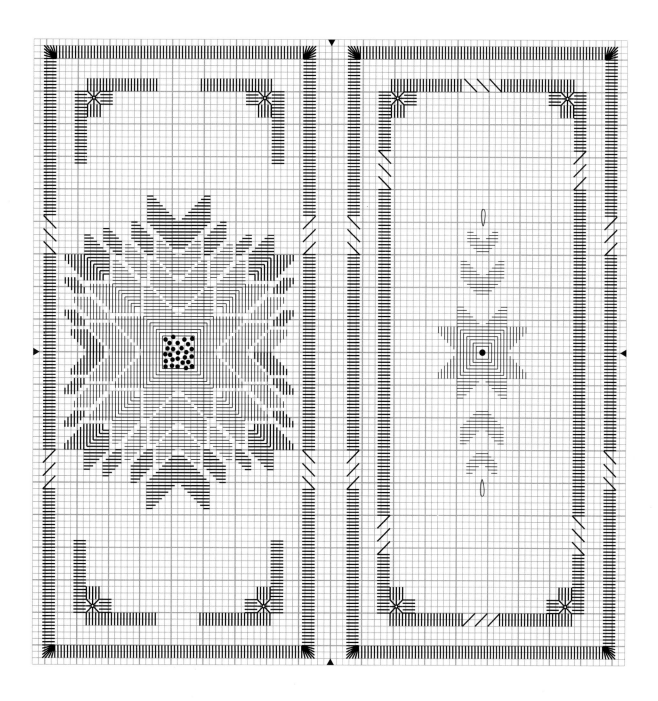

YOU WILL NEED

- [ ] 18 gauge, Zweigart Davosa 9 ½in (24.5cm) x 15in (38.5cm)
- [ ] DMC stranded cotton yellow or gold
- [ ] DMC 3 perlé white
- [ ] DMC 12 perlé
- [ ] Kreinik 32 metallic braid red and gold
- [ ] Kreinik 16 metallic braid red
- [ ] tapestry needle 20/120 or 22/130
- [ ] dressmaker's thread
- [ ] paper punch
- [ ] red ribbon
- [ ] embroidery hoop or frame

Stitch chart
1 square = 2 fabric threads

1 White poinsettia book cover. This design features a single poinsettia worked on 18 gauge even weave fabric. It is worked in a Victorian Christmas green with ornate French knots for the central flowers. The white of the poinsettia is worked in DMC 3 perlé in satin stitch. The outer ring of leaves is worked in Kreinik 32 metallic braid gold, with running stitch at the top and bottom. The white poinsettias are edged in straight stitch using Kreinik 32 metallic braid red. Follow making up instructions from step 4 of the red book cover (page 64).

2 Place punched papers inside the book, and thread with two lengths of red ribbon, through both the fabric and pages, then tie in bows.

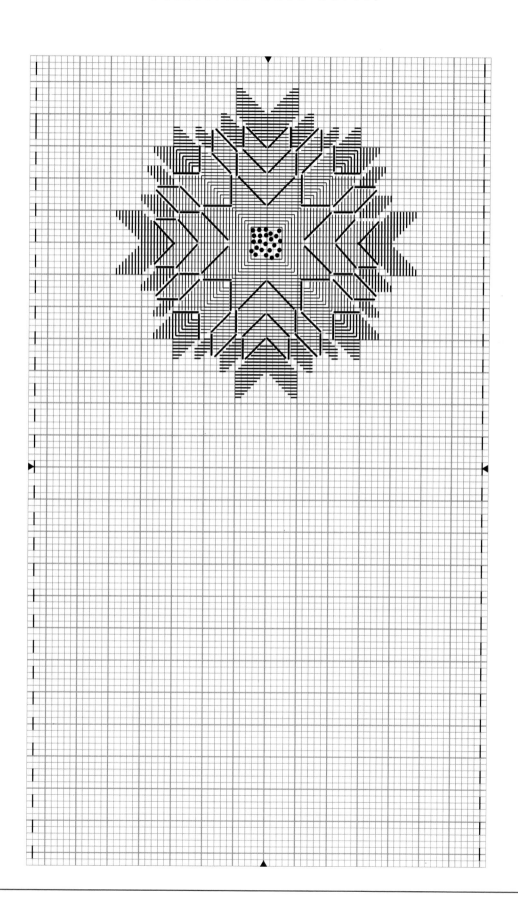

POINSETTIA BOOK MARKS

The book mark is a small embroidered motif attached to a hand twisted cord with a matching tassel at the end. The embroidered square uses an attractive design which matches the book cover. What a wonderful, festive combination as a gift for a loved one.

1 **Red poinsettia book mark 1**. Cut a piece of fabric and fit it in the hoop or frame. Find the centre of the fabric and mark it with tacking stitches.

2 Work the red poinsettia, following the chart in DMC 3 perlé red. The centre flowers are worked in gold or yellow French knots. Each corner features a red bud worked out of a central hole. The leaves around each bud are worked in satin stitch with DMC 5 perlé green. The border is worked in buttonhole stitch using DMC 5 perlé green, with the looped portion of the stitch on the edge of the square.

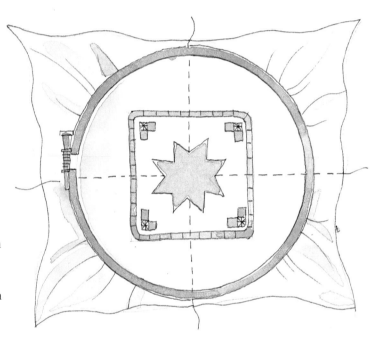

YOU WILL NEED

- ☐ tapestry needle 20 or 22
- ☐ dressmaker's thread
- ☐ embroidery hoop or frame
- ☐ twisted cord
- ☐ tassel

Red poinsettia book mark 1
- ☐ 20 gauge, Zweigart Valerie 4in (10cm) square, mushroom
- ☐ DMC stranded cotton yellow
- ☐ DMC 3 perlé green
- ☐ DMC 5 perlé red

Red poinsettia book mark 2
- ☐ 20 gauge, Zweigart Valerie 4in (10cm) square, mushroom
- ☐ DMC stranded cotton yellow
- ☐ DMC 3 perlé green
- ☐ DMC 5 perlé red

White poinsettia book mark
- ☐ 20 gauge, Zweigart Davosa 4in (10cm) square
- ☐ DMC 3 perlé white
- ☐ DMC 3 perlé green

- ☐ Kreinik 32 metallic braid gold
- ☐ Kreinik 16 metallic braid red

When you've finished working you may find it helpful to use a fine line of fabric glue along the edge, which will control unruly loose threads.

Stitch chart
1 square = 2 fabric threads

3 When the embroidery is complete, couch a DMC 3 perlé green thread to the edge of the square. Work button hole stitch over the green thread.

4 Remove the fabric from the hoop or frame and carefully cut away the excess fabric using small sharp scissors. Cut as closely to the stitching as possible without cutting into any stitching.

5 Make up the cord and tassel and attach the cord to one corner of the square. The hand-twisted cord is 14in (36cm) long, made from a twisted pair of DMC 3 perlé green. The tassel is made from DMC 3 perlé red, and is 3in (7.7cm) long. Attach the tassel to the end of the cord and then fix the cord securely to the book mark.

6 **Red poinsettia book mark 2**. Work the same as the first bookmark following the second chart. The yellow flowers in the centre are worked in French knots. Finish off the book mark following steps 3-5.

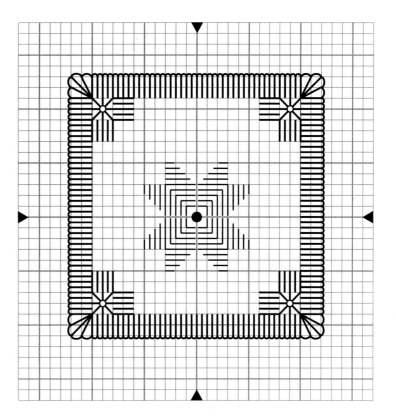

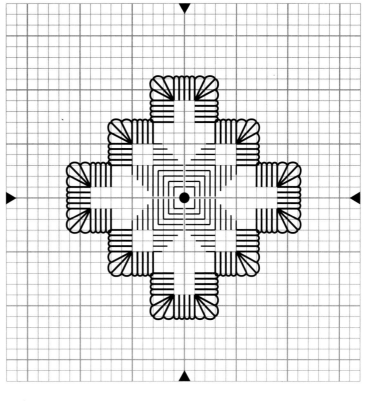

7 **White poinsettia book mark.** The book mark is worked in a 20 count even weave square with a trailing twisted cord and tassel. The poinsettia and colours match the colours and design of the white poinsettia book cover. The white poinsettia is worked in DMC 3 perlé in satin stitch, with the central flowers in French knots of Kreinik 16 metallic braid red. Surround the white poinsettia with satin stitch worked in Kreinik 32 metallic braid gold. Finish off following steps 3-5.

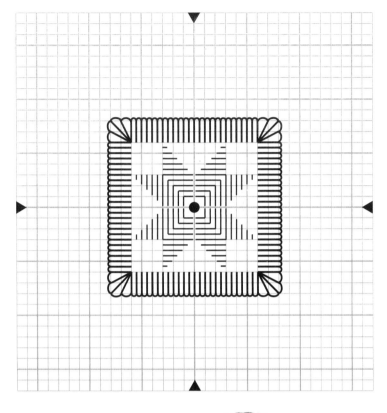

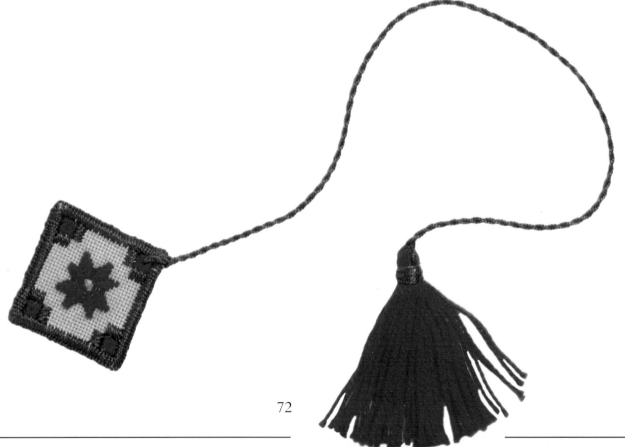

THE CHRISTMAS ROSE CUSHION

With a lovely, full-blown, golden rose surrounded by a bouquet of red, gold and white rose buds, this cushion will be the lifelong treasured possession of someone dear. Trimmed with detached chain stitches and cord that loops and curls across the top, this project uses a variety of techniques to beautiful effect.

1 **The small roses.** Fold the ribbon over to make a 90° angle across itself. Roll the folded ribbon from the smallest side until it meets the 90° angle. Make a couple of stitches through the bottom edge to secure the roll.

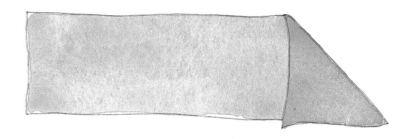

YOU WILL NEED

- [ ] cotton or silk fabric 2 x 9in (23cm) square
- [ ] wadding 9in (23cm) square
- [ ] cushion pad 8in (20cm) square
- [ ] wire edged gold silk ribbon 1yd (1m) of 1 ½in (39mm) wide
- [ ] wide red, white and gold ribbon 12in (31cm)–18in (46cm) each of 1 ½in (39mm)
- [ ] green silk ribbon 1yd (1m) of ⅜in (9mm) wide
- [ ] decorative cord 2yds (2m)
- [ ] gold cord 1yd (1m)
- [ ] sharp needle
- [ ] dressmaker's thread
- [ ] hand stitching metallic thread
- [ ] scissors
- [ ] pins

2 Again, fold the ribbon across itself forming a 90° angle. Reposition the ribbon in your hand so that it is held at the angle indicated.

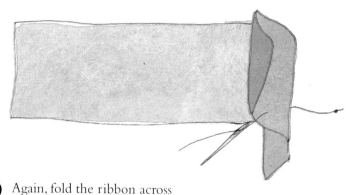

3 Roll from the smallest edge a couple of turns until the edge meets the 90° angle. Take a couple of stitches at the bottom edge to secure the roll. Continue to fold and roll the ribbon until the rose grows to the size you want. Stitch the final roll in place. Make three red, three white and two gold roses.

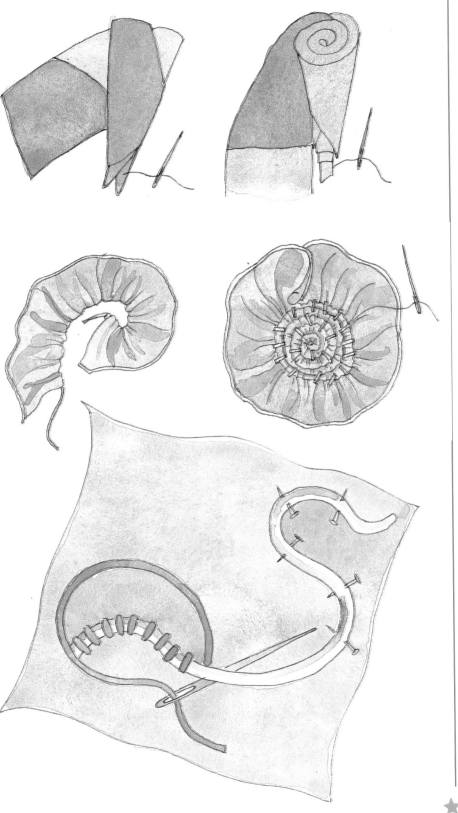

4 **The full bloom.** Gather the gold wired ribbon along one side of the wire until it occupies ⅓ of the wire's length. Turn in the raw edge and manipulate the ribbon so that the gathered portion forms a spiral. Start with a few tight turns in the centre, increasing the diameter as the ribbon is wound together. As you work, take a few stitches to secure the spiral. To finish, turn the raw edge under the bloom, and stitch it to secure the shape. Leave the thread and needle attached.

5 **Attaching the cord.** Position the cord over the top of the cushion and pin it in place. Couch the cord down to the cushion fabric using a hand stitching metallic thread, or a gold coloured, strong cotton thread (see Couched Threads on page 76).

6 **Attaching roses to cushion cover.** Position and pin the roses in the positions shown on the illustration. Start with the large bloom. When you are happy with their position, stitch the base of the blooms to the cushion front. Let roses overlap each other to make a nice compact arrangement. Work detached chain stitch outward, from the base of the blooms using the ⅜in (9mm) ribbon.

7 Place the front and back of the cushion right sides together. Pin, then stitch firmly using hand or machine stitching. Leave a 6in (15cm) gap to turn through. Turn the cushion cover right-side out.

8 Insert the pad inside the cushion cover. Hand stitch the opening to close the cushion.

9 Couch the cord around the edge of the cushion, covering the seams, and leaving loops at the corners, and in the middle of the edges if you wish. There is more information on corded edges on page 104.

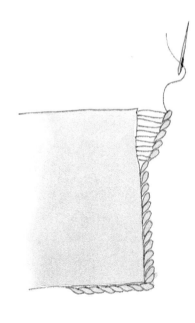

COUCHED THREADS

Heavy metallic threads and other decorative threads are sometimes too heavy to work with a needle. They are better worked using the couched thread technique. To couch a heavy cord, bring the cord up to the front of the fabric. Lay the cord along an edge, design line, or in the position desired, and pin it in place. Bring a finer thread to the surface and stitch, crossing the cord at right angles, working along the full length of the couched thread. Stitch at ¼in (0.5cm) intervals. Use this method to apply heavy cords, braid, and threads.

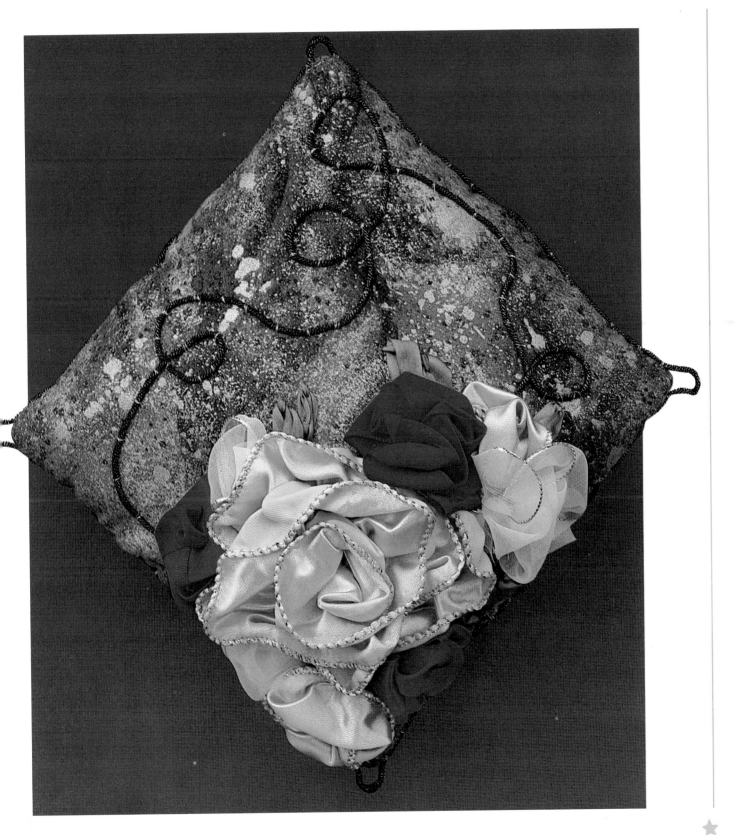

CHRISTMAS ROSE PHOTO FRAME

With the beauty of the rose and ribbons, threads and cords, many lovely needlework techniques work in combination. When these elements serve to frame a personal portrait, or family photo, it makes a gift to be cherished as a family heirloom.

YOU WILL NEED

- ☐ cotton fabric 3 pieces 6½in (16.5) x 7½in (19cm);2 pieces 5in (13cm) x 3 ¾in (9.5cm)
- ☐ cotton wadding 2 pieces 5 ¼in (13.5cm) x 6 ¼in (16.2cm); 1 piece 2 ¾in (7cm) x 3 ¾in (9.5cm); 1 piece 6 ½in (16.5cm) x 7 ½in (19.2cm)
- ☐ heavy card 1 piece 5 ⅛in (13.2cm) x 6 ⅛in (16cm); 1 piece 5 ¼in (13.5cm) x 6 ¼in (16.2cm); 1 piece 1 ½in (4cm) wide at the top, 3in (7.7cm) wide at the bottom x 4in (10cm) high
- ☐ sharp needle
- ☐ dressmaker's thread
- ☐ marker pen
- ☐ ruler
- ☐ glue
- ☐ scissors
- ☐ pins

Decorative Threads Needed
- ☐ 3 yds (3m) x ¾in (2cm) round metallic cord gold couched for stems and to finish off both inner and outer edge of frame with slip stitch
- ☐ dressmaker's thread in gold colour couching stitches for above braid
- ☐ Kreinik 16 metallic braid gold running stitch for stems and branch effects
- ☐ 1yd (1m) x ¾in (2cm) wide metallic wire ribbon gold folded and turned to make roses
- ☐ 1 yd (1m) x ¼in (7mm) silk ribbon red folded and turned to make roses
- ☐ 2 yds (2m) x ¼in (7mm) wide silk ribbon gold chain stitch roses with French knots
- ☐ 1yd (1m) x ⅛in (4mm) wide silk ribbon red rosebuds in detached chain stitch
- ☐ 1yd (1m) x ¼in (7mm) wide silk ribbon green straight stitch leaves around gold folded and turned roses

- ☐ 2yds (2m) x ⅟₁₆in (2mm) silk ribbon green straight stitch leaves surrounding rose buds and all other flowers

Stitches. Ribbon work stitches (page 11). Straight stitch, French knot, chain stitch (pages 19–20).

1 **Cutting the card to make the frame**. Find the centre of the front card and measure for a picture cut-out. Measure 1 ⅜in (3.5cm) to the right and left of the vertical centre line. Measure up from the horizontal line 2in (5cm), and measure down 1 ¾in (4.5cm). Before cutting, check to ensure the cut-out measures 2 ¾in (7cm) x 3 ¾in (9.5cm). If the measurement is correct, cut the hole in the card. Cut the hinge from a piece of card, ½in (4cm) wide at the top, 3in (7.7cm) wide at the bottom and 4in (10cm) high. Do the same with a piece of wadding.

2 **Preparing fabric for embroidery**. Lay the fabric for the front of the frame on top of the wadding cut to 5 ¼in (13.5cm) x 6 ¼in (16.2cm), and tack into place. The wadding helps to prevent the fabric puckering when embroidery stitches are applied. Mark the stitching areas with running stitches which will be removed later. Trace the hinge card on the 3¾ in (9.5cm) x 5in (13cm) fabric, allowing a ⅝in (1.5cm) hem allowance beyond the edges of the card.

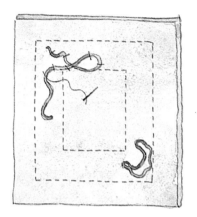

3 **Rose and stitching placement.** Lay the dark metallic cord on the fabric along the stitched lines. Pin the cord in position at the top left and bottom right of the frame. These are the meandering branches that create a guide for placing the flowers and leaves. Couch these cords in place using a matching dressmaker's thread.

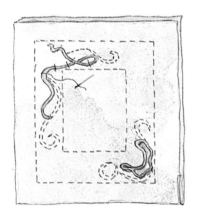

4 Continue the development of the meandering branches and stems in running stitch using Kreinik 16 metallic braid gold.

5 **Making the roses.** Make the two largest roses first. Using the ¾in (2cm) wide gold metallic ribbon, make the roses following the folded and turned method described in steps 1–3 of the Christmas rose cushion project (page 74). The diameter of the roses will be about 2 ⅛in (5.5cm). Stitch the roses to the frame at the top left and bottom right hand corners. Make straight stitches surrounding the roses with ¼in (7mm) wide green silk ribbon. Place the leaves and flowers close together, and overlap cords and running stitches in some places.

6 **Finished stitch placement.** Fix roses, gold, silk, detached chain stitch roses, red silk rosebuds, and green leaves, in position. Use your eye to position them as you like, using the illustration as a guide, and add extra flowers or leaves as you see fit. At this point, the cords shown around the edges and centre opening have not been added.

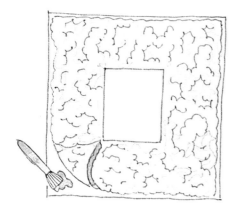

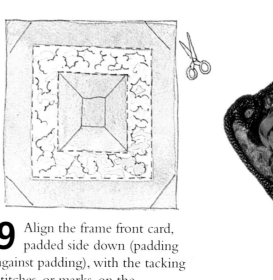

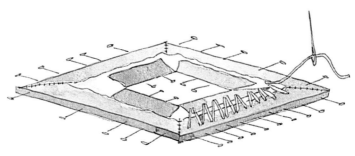

7 **Frame front construction.** Apply a light coating of glue to frame front. Carefully position the wadding over the card. Set aside to dry.

9 Align the frame front card, padded side down (padding against padding), with the tacking stitches, or marks, on the embroidered front fabric. Trim the corners of the fabric as indicated in the illustration.

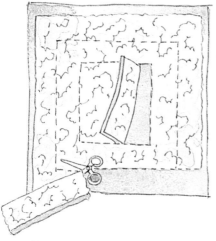

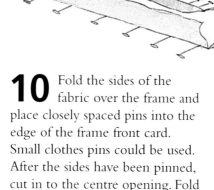

8 Lay out the embroidered front fabric with padded side uppermost. Align the frame front card as close as possible to the tacking stitches on the fabric. If they do not line up, draw a light pencil line around the frame to show the frame edges, both the cut-out and the outside edges. Carefully cut back the padding around the edges of the card, including the hole in the centre. Do not cut the embroidered fabric at this stage.

10 Fold the sides of the fabric over the frame and place closely spaced pins into the edge of the frame front card. Small clothes pins could be used. After the sides have been pinned, cut in to the centre opening. Fold the fabric over the card, and pin it in place.

11 With a needle and strong dressmaker's thread, lace the outside edges to the inside edges, working opposing joins of fabric to achieve an even tension all round the frame. Mitre out side corners, and cut away any excess fabric to reduce bulk.

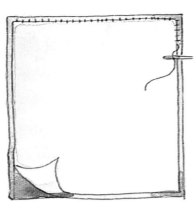

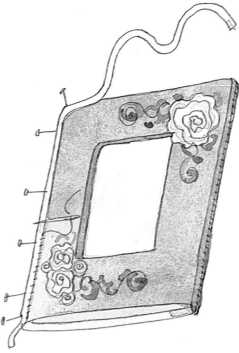

12 **Picture frame assembly.** An optional cord or braid could be added to the edges of the picture opening in the frame front. If you want to do this add it now. Insert the tip of the cord between the fabric and card. Pin it in place, and slip stitch around the opening to secure the cord.

14 Lay the lining fabric on an ironing board and press the edges under to make a small hem. The fabric should now be slightly smaller than the backing. Lay the lining over the backing card and slip stitch it in place.

16 Align the frame front and frame back making sure any size difference is compensated equally, from side to side, or top to bottom. Attach the front to the back with a matching thread, making small slip stitches. Leave the top edge open so you can insert a photograph. The frame could be further embellished through the addition of a cord or braid around the outer edge. Arrange the cord or braid around the outer edge of the front frame card and pin it in place. Slip stitch the cord to secure it to the frame.

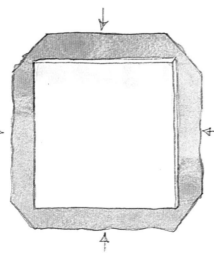

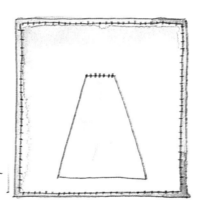

13 Place the previously cut backing card on top of the backing fabric. Turn the edges of the fabric over the back of the card and secure firmly with a little glue.

15 Stitch the small pieces of hinge fabric together around three sides, leaving the bottom edge open. Insert the hinge card between the fabric layers and close the opening using slip stitch. Stitch the hinge piece to the backing card so that the frame back stands comfortably by itself.

HANGING HEART PHOTO FRAME

Whether you're near to home or far away, nothing makes Christmas more special than the sight of a loved one, even if it can only be in a photo. This special felt heart frame is decorated with simple stitches. You can adapt this project to fit in with the amount of time you have available to work it.

1 Lay the piece of felt over a piece of interfacing. Choose the method you would like to use to decorate the fabric. Any zig-zag, utility, or decorative stitch available on the machine will work well or use hand stitching. There is no need to back stitch to secure threads. Arcing and swooping lines are quick to work and the finished look is effective. A few strands or ribbons could be couched on to the fabric by hand or machine.

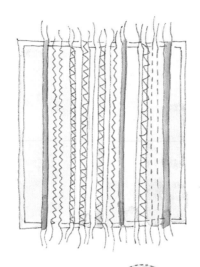

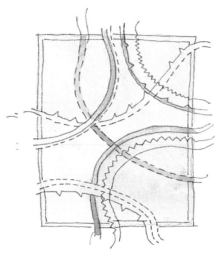

YOU WILL NEED

- [ ] felt 2 pieces 8in (20cm) square
- [ ] interfacing 1 x 9in (23cm) square
- [ ] iron-on interfacing 1 x 8in (20cm) square
- [ ] machine embroidery thread 3 colours to match felt
- [ ] Kreinik 16 metallic braid 3 colours
- [ ] wired ribbon
- [ ] 10 small button
- [ ] needle
- [ ] dressmaker's thread
- [ ] marker pen
- [ ] paper
- [ ] double-sided sticky tape

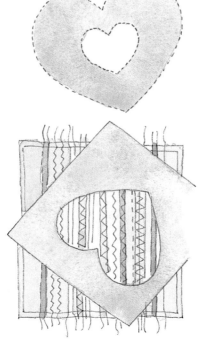

2 Enlarge the heart shape until it measures 5 ⅞in (14.8cm) across. Make a further heart shape 2 ⅜in (6cm) across. Cut the enlarged shapes from the paper.

3 Using the paper from which the larger heart shape was cut, place the heart shaped hole over the stitching. Place it over a pleasing area of stitching, then mark the outline using a fabric marker. Centre the small heart shape over the larger on the fabric, and mark this shape too. Straight stitch over both outlines.

4 With sharp scissors, cut out the large heart shape from the stitched fabric. Carefully cut out the small heart shape from the centre. Machine a narrow zig-zag stitch over all the raw edges.

5 Work buttonhole stitch around the front edge of the inner heart shape. Sew on the buttons for added detail, using a variety of stitch techniques. Use double-sided sticky tape to fix photo behind the cut-out.

6 Press a piece of iron-on interfacing on to the second piece of felt. Trace the large heart shape on to the felt and cut it out carefully.

7 Align the 2 large heart shapes, wrong sides together, and pin them in place.

8 **Hand stitching edges.** Starting from the centre cleft of the heart, stitch front and back together using a button hole stitch. For a fuller appearance, insert a needle under the bars of the button hole stitch and work another thread through them. As the stitching returns to the top point, leave a loop of thread from which to hang the frame. For a firmer edge, work a second row of buttonholing around the edge.

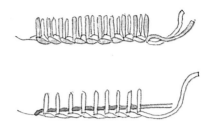

9 **Finishing.** Make a small bow of wired ribbon and fix it to the top of the larger heart.

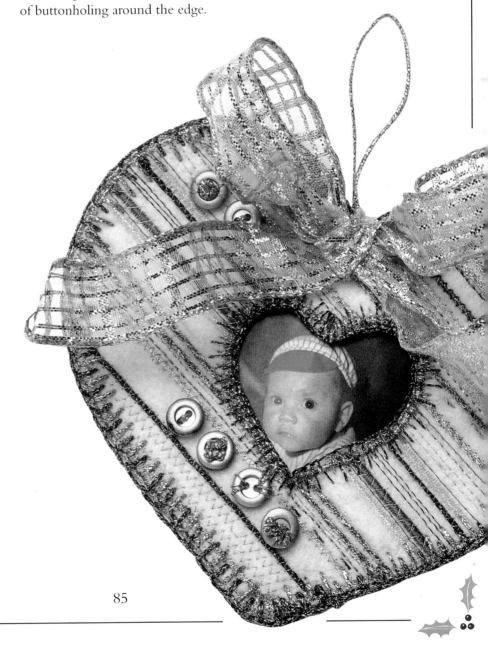

GIFT CONTAINER

The circle is an ancient source of inspiration for a wide range of design themes and articles. Here, it is used to create a small gift container which is almost a gift in itself. The design could also be made into a small round cloth to decorate a festive table.

1 Cut 8 pieces of 4in (10cm) long ribbon. Thread a ribbon through the loop at the top of each bell and set aside.

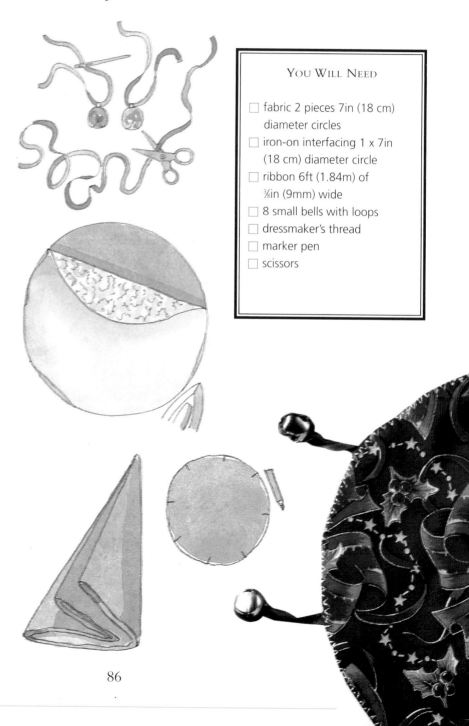

YOU WILL NEED

- [ ] fabric 2 pieces 7in (18 cm) diameter circles
- [ ] iron-on interfacing 1 x 7in (18 cm) diameter circle
- [ ] ribbon 6ft (1.84m) of ⅜in (9mm) wide
- [ ] 8 small bells with loops
- [ ] dressmaker's thread
- [ ] marker pen
- [ ] scissors

2 Lay the interfacing with the adhesive surface against the wrong side of one of the fabric circles, and press with a moderately hot iron (not too hot for fabric).

3 Fold the fabric circle in half and press. Fold the circle again, into quarters, and press. Fold once more and press again. Open the fabric up to the right side which will now have eight segments. Mark the edge of each segment with a marker pencil. The marks will indicate the point at which each of the bells should be attached.

4 Mark a small seam allowance around the edge of the circle. Use this as a guide line for pinning the bell ribbons to the fabric. Pin them to the positions marked with the bells pointing towards the centre of the circle.

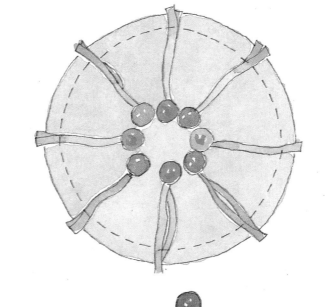

5 Position the second fabric circle on top of the first, right sides together, and pin in position. Stitch around the edge of the circle leaving a 2in (5cm) gap through which the circle, with bells attached, can be turned inside out. Carefully turn the piece inside out and press the seam.

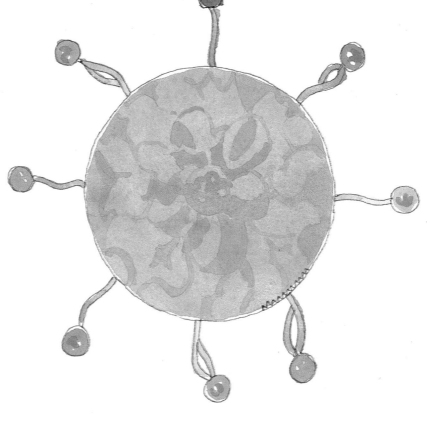

6 Using either straight stitch or a decorative zig-zag, sew around the edge of the circle to finish off the edge.

7 Bring together a pair of neighbouring bell ribbons and tie the two ribbons together with a reef knot. Repeat this all around the circle with the remaining three neighbouring pairs. This will make a four-cornered container.

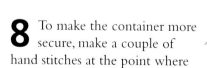

8 To make the container more secure, make a couple of hand stitches at the point where each pair of ribbons is tied.

VARIATIONS

Bell circle. Divide the circle evenly into sixteen segments and thread a bell on to a ribbon for each segment. Pin the fabric at every other bell to see the different shapes you can achieve with different bell pairings.

Larger container. A larger fabric circle will create a bigger container. Use a stiffer fabric for larger circles.

Cornucopia. Make the circle into a cone shape and tie some of the bells together. Insert a sprig of holly or ivy in the opening.

CHRISTMAS TREE SKIRT

The Christmas tree is one of the most dominant symbols of Christmas. This project provides a lovely covering for the unsightly tree base and stand. It is padded and lined so it can be reversed on alternating years, to give a fresh perspective.

YOU WILL NEED

- [ ] printed fabric 3½ yds (3.25m) of 45in (115cm) wide for the skirt
- [ ] printed fabric 1yd (1m) of 45in (115cm) wide for the belled straps
- [ ] lining 3½yds (3.25m) of 45in (115cm) wide
- [ ] light wadding 3yds (3.22m)
- [ ] Madeira metallic thread
- [ ] Kreinik 32 metallic braid gold 11yds (10.1m)
- [ ] bias tape
- [ ] needle
- [ ] dressmaker's thread
- [ ] marker pen
- [ ] scissors

The skirt pattern for this project is 56in (143cm) in diameter which would be suitable for a tree of 6-7 feet (1.84-2.15m) in height. For a smaller tree, decrease the measurements according to the area requirements.

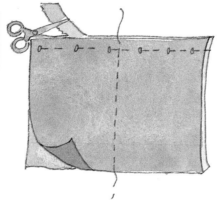

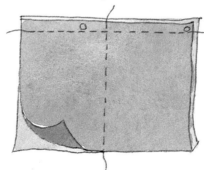

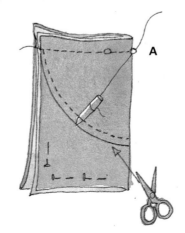

1 Top fabric. Cut 2 pieces of fabric, 45in x 56in (115cm x 143cm). Pin the right sides together. Cut 1in (2.5cm) from the selvedges at the top edge. Mark the centre point at the top. Tack along the top half way and machine stitch the other half. Find the centre of the fabric and, working from top to bottom, tack the two fabric layers

2 Lining. Find the centre of the fabric and tack the two layers together from top to bottom. Mark the centre point at the top. Allowing a 1in (2.5cm) seam allowance, machine stitch half the top seam, and tack the remainder.

3 Top fabric and lining. (instructions are the same for both) Fold the fabric in half along the tacked line. Smooth and flatten the layers. Insert a few pins to secure the fabric. At point (A), insert a pin to which a string can be anchored. Tie a piece of string to the pin and at a point 28in (72cm) (27in [69cm] for lining) down the string, tie a fabric marker or pencil. Holding the marker taut, draw an arc on the fabric. Cut the fabric along the line of the arc.

4 Unfold the fabric into a semi-circle. Remove the tacking thread. Take a small stitch to mark the centre point on each side. Repeat for the lining.

5 Unfold the fabric into a full circle. Press the seam open and ensure the centre stitch marker is visible. Repeat for the lining.

6 **Lining and wadding.** Cut the wadding 1in (2.5cm) larger all around than the lining fabric. Lay the lining fabric right side up, on top of the wadding. Tack from the centre outwards to securely mate the lining to the wadding. When completed, trim the wadding back to the edge of the lining fabric, making both the same diameter.

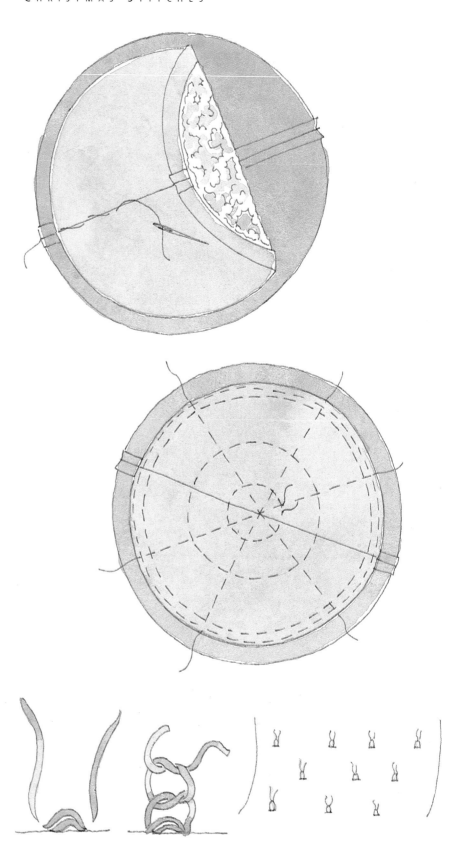

7 **Joining layers.** Lay out the top fabric with the right side facing down. Carefully align the padded lining fabric on top, matching the seams and placing the tacked seams on top of each other. The top fabric should be 1in (2.5cm) larger all around than the lining. Using the centre marker, find the exact centre point and securely tack the layers together working from the centre towards the edges.

8 From the centre point, use the string and pencil to mark an inner circle with a 6 ½in (16.5cm) diameter. Work a line of tacking stitches around this circle. Work a couple more concentric circles of tacking stitches, spaced equidistantly, between the centre and the edge.

9 **Tied quilting.** This technique can be used to give additional character to the skirt and further secure the layers. Use a matching thread DMC 12 perlé or a few strands of stranded cotton. Thread the needle, but do not tie a knot at the end of the thread. Take the needle through all the fabric layers, and repeat the stitch in the same spot. Leave enough tail to make a knot. Tie a reef knot and clip the threads leaving a small tuft. To arrange ties, measure along a line and make a dot about every 6in (15cm). Working on the lining side of the skirt, make stitches at the dots.

10 **Finishing.** Cut out the previously marked hole in the centre of the skirt, leaving the tacking threads around the hole in place. Remove the tacking stitches along one seam of both top fabric and lining fabric. You can now cut the wadding along the seam line from the edge to the centre. The skirt will now open along one side.

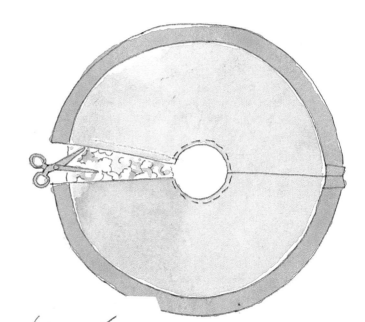

11 Trim the wadding along the seam. Turn under the raw edges at the side opening. Pin and tack the edges together.

12 Fold over the raw edges of the top fabric. Pin and tack the turned edge to the lining fabric and slip stitch them together. Apply bias tape over the stitched edges of the side opening.

13 **Bell straps.** Cut six strips of the fabric into pieces 6in (15cm) x 25in (64cm). Fold then in half along the length with the wrong side out. Stitch along the straps leaving a 3in (7.7cm) opening. Position the strap so the seam runs down the centre of it. Mark off, and stitch a pointed shape at the ends of the straps. Trim the excess fabric. Press the seam open. Turn the strap inside out to show the right side of the fabric. Slipstitch the opening.

14 Pin and stitch the straps into position around the central opening of the skirt. Position one strap over the side opening to conceal the opening. To make detachable straps, stitch large bells or tassels to the ends of each. Gold thread or braid could be stitched to the edges to add glitter and colour.

15 Alternatively you could leave the Christmas tree skirt plain without stitching, quilting, or straps.

CARAFE COVER

*A quick and easy, yet decorative cloth to drape over an open container or carafe.
The dangling buttons and beads provide a nice weight to the cloth which helps
to hold it in position. If you like, you could paint the buttons to match
the carafe cover.*

1 Attaching buttons. Buttons can be attached in any number of decorative and unusual ways. Try using metallic threads, or other strong, lustrous, colourful thread. Stitch the button in the corners by taking a thread through one of the thread holes, around the edge of the button, and work buttonhole stitch along the thread. Do this for each thread hole, or add more stitches through the same hole. Make French knots over the thread holes. Alternatively, work straight stitches through the holes, out over the edges, and into the cloth. Use a decorative thread to make an 'X' over the button or thread some beads on to the needle so they will lie across the top of the button.

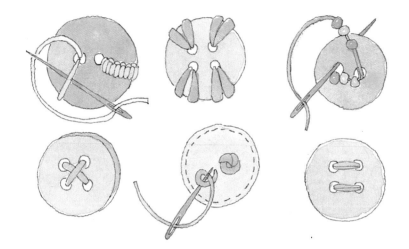

2 Dangling buttons over the edges. Take a couple of stitches to secure the thread in the edge of the cloth, or work a few buttonhole stitches, before picking up the button. Return the thread from the button to the cloth, passing through any other buttons on the thread.

3 Work buttonhole stitch on the return journey along the attaching thread, to strengthen the thread. Secure the end, by working a few stitches at the edge of the cloth.

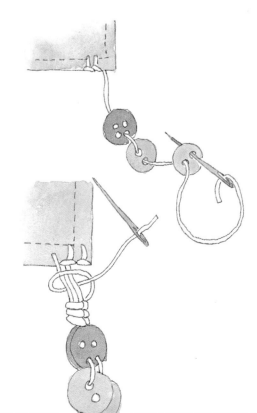

YOU WILL NEED

- ☐ cotton fabric 10in (25.5cm) square
- ☐ buttons
- ☐ gold braid
- ☐ needle
- ☐ dressmaker's thread
- ☐ scissors

LITTLE BUTTON CLOTH

Here is another easy-to-make, festive little cloth for Christmas. Take fifty buttons from your button jar and paint them gold with spray paint. Use the cloth as a centre piece on your festive table, or as cloth upon which to place a candlestick or decorative arrangement.

1 Take the two fabric pieces and place them right sides together. Stitch around the edges leaving a small gap through which to turn them. Trim excess fabric around the edge and turn the fabric inside out.

2 Work up and down buttonhole, around the edge of the fabric. Begin like ordinary buttonhole stitch, pulling the thread through the fabric. Then insert the needle under the edge of the material, and take an upward stitch.

> ### YOU WILL NEED
>
> ☐ fabric 2 pieces 4 ⅝in (11.8cm) diameter circles
> ☐ Kreinik 8 metallic braid or DMC 8 perlé
> ☐ needle
> ☐ dressmaker's thread
> ☐ buttons
> ☐ scissors

3 The thread will now be lying under the point of the needle. Ease the needle and thread upwards and then down, to make the stitch. Continue working like this around the edge of the fabric. Ordinary buttonhole stitch could be substituted here.

4 After completion, take a new thread, and add buttons as the needle is worked in and out of the buttonhole loops at the edge of the fabric. Wrap the shank as the buttons are added.

CIRCULAR TABLECLOTH

The circular tablecloth creates a foundation for a whole series of table settings as you can use layers of different sized cloths in complementary colours with matching, complementary or contrasting napkins to complete the effect. Changing the top cloth creates a new atmosphere.

1 Working out fabric size.
This depends of the size of the table on which it will be used. Measure the diameter of the table top. Then measure from the edge of the table top, down a leg, the distance the cloth should fall. You could make the cloth to reach the floor. Take the diameter of the table, and add twice the length of the desired fall to give you the length; you will need two lengths of fabric.

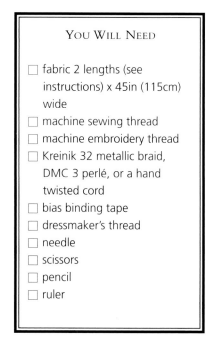

YOU WILL NEED

☐ fabric 2 lengths (see instructions) x 45in (115cm) wide
☐ machine sewing thread
☐ machine embroidery thread
☐ Kreinik 32 metallic braid, DMC 3 perlé, or a hand twisted cord
☐ bias binding tape
☐ dressmaker's thread
☐ needle
☐ scissors
☐ pencil
☐ ruler

2 With fabric measuring 45in (115cm) in width, the cloth will require two widths to make 90in (2.3m). To avoid a seam in the middle of the cloth, cut one piece in half along its length. Sew one strip on either side of the remaining 45in (115cm) wide piece. The resulting piece of fabric will be a 90in (2.3m) square. Turn the cloth to the wrong side and press both the seams open flat.

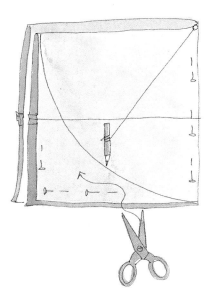

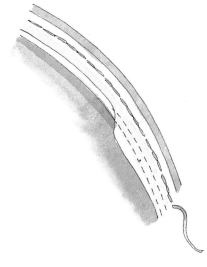

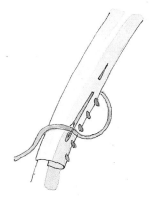

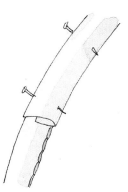

3 Carefully fold the cloth in half, and fold it in half again, so that the centre of the cloth is in one corner of the resulting square. Draw an arc from the centre point connecting the outer corners.

4 Bias tape binding is used to finish the edge of the circular table cloth. Dotted lines indicate folds in the tape fabric. Mate the edges of the binding tape and tablecloth fabric, right sides together. Tack along the outermost fold line on the bias tape, joining the tape to the table cloth fabric. This will secure the fabric from stretching while machine stitching the edge. Set the machine for straight stitch and stitch alongside the line of tacking stitches. When finished, remove the tacking stitches.

5 Turn the cloth over to the back. Fold the binding tape over the edge. Pin the binding tape to the back of the table cloth, just covering the machine stitched line showing through to the back of the tablecloth.

6 Attach the bias tape to the back of the cloth using hand sewn slip stitch.

7 **Table napkins or square or rectangular cloth.** To match your cloth make napkins, 14in (36cm) x 14in (36cm). Work the rolled edges by machine and finish off with a cord, using Kreinik 32 metallic braid gold (see page 104).

CARDINAL POINTS TABLECLOTH

If jolly old Saint Nick ever gets lost on his midnight ride from the North Pole,
he could pull out his Cardinal points tablecloth and compass to help him to
find his way. The finely tapered points on this cloth look good on a round table,
draped over a matching or complementary round tablecloth.

1 Start with a 45in (115cm) square of fabric. Fold the square in half diagonally to creat a triangle, press along the crease. Fold in half again, and press.

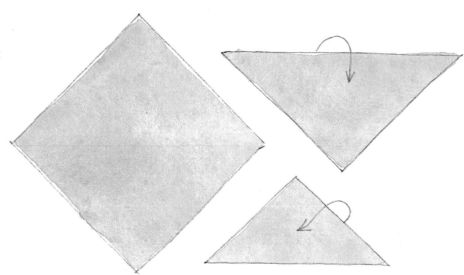

YOU WILL NEED

- ☐ patterned fabric 45in (115cm) square
- ☐ tassels
- ☐ ribbon
- ☐ needle
- ☐ dressmaker's thread
- ☐ marker pen
- ☐ ruler
- ☐ counterweight

2 Fold again, press along the crease. Turn the triangular bundle so the folded edges face left, and the triangle forms a right angle on the left. Measure up the edge and fold over at 6 ¾in (17cm) from the corner.

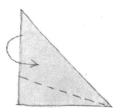

3 Unfold the fabric, and, with a straight edge, draw a line from the previous mark out towards the corners. Cut carefully along the lines and remove the excess fabric.

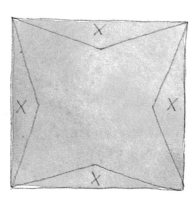

4 **Finishing.** Refer to the section on machine stitched rolled edges (page 104), and use it to finish the edges.

5 **Tablecloth tassels.** Attach a tassel to one or both ends of a ribbon. Pin or stitch in place. If you want to make a feature of a single giant tassel, place a counterweight on the opposite end of the ribbon (refer to tassel project page 110 for instructions to make a tassel).

6 Arrange the tassels over a circular cloth overlaid with the cardinal points tablecloth. Arrange the tassels so they align with the points of the cloth. Although it may seem as if the tassels are fastened to the tablecloth, they are actually hanging on ribbons. The arrangement will work for almost any tablecloth, or even a simple cloth square.

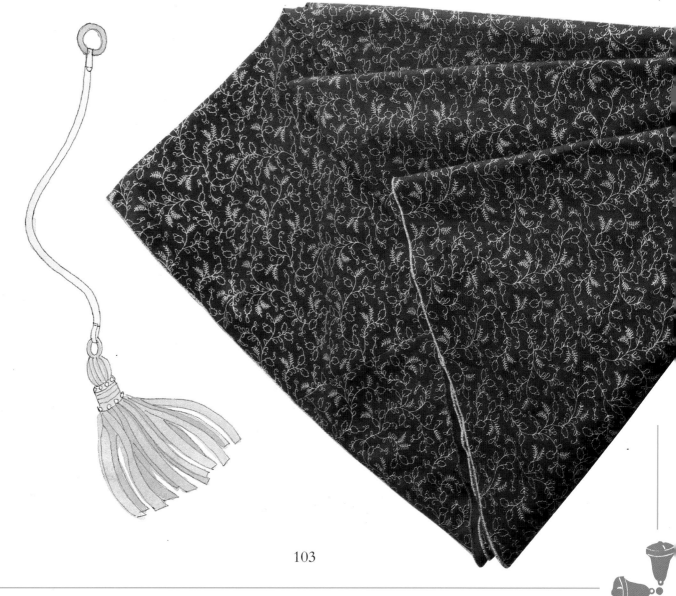

1 **Rolled edges by machine.** The rolled edge is one of the nicest finishing techniques for squares, rectangles and the cardinal points tablecloth. Work a trial piece on a small piece of fabric to learn the technique and gain confidence before working on the project piece. Starch the fabric before making the edge.

2 **Set up the machine as follows:** *Top tension:* Set tension on the universal setting. *Top thread:* Matching machine embroidery thread. *Bobbin thread:* Matching colour. *Needle:* Embroidery or universal type, size 11/75-12/80. *Stitch setting:* Straight stitch. *Stitch length:* 2mm. *Foot:* Standard sewing foot.

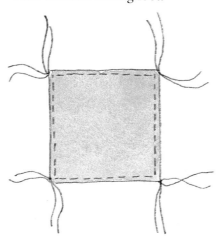

3 Position the cloth under the machine foot about ⅛in (3mm) from the edge. Leave long tail threads at the start, and end of each corner. The tails will be used as hand holds to help manipulate the fabric on corner turns. Stitch along each side, repositioning the fabric under the needle at each corner of the square.

4 Change the sewing foot to a satin stitch or embroidery foot. Set the stitch width to ⅛in (3mm), and shorten the stitch length, making stitches slightly closer together. Position the fabric under the foot and adjust the fabric so that the needle produces the zig-zag stitch just outside the edge of the fabric on the alternate swing of the needle.

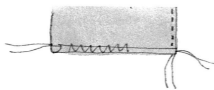

5 Begin stitching from a point a little beyond the corner. As you stitch, the edge of the fabric should begin to curl and roll under. If it does not, increase top tension, or slightly lengthen the zig-zag. As you approach the corners, hold the thread tails and pull slight tension on them to keep the fabric taut. It is important to use a matching machine embroidery thread.

6 **Adding cord or braid to the edge by machine.** Use a stiff, rounded cord that is not too limp, such as Kreinik 32 metallic braid, DMC 3 perlé, or a hand twisted cord. Set up your machine as follows: *Top and bobbin threads:* Machine embroidery threads to match the cord. *Needle:* Metafil, machine embroidery needle, or a top stitch needle, size 12/80-14/90. *Foot:* Embroidery or cording foot. *Stitch width:* 3.5mm.

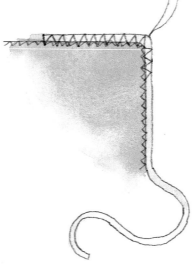

7 Position the cord and fabric so that the needle swings slightly beyond the cord and back across the previous stitching. It should butt up against the fabric. Stitch around the material to secure the cord.

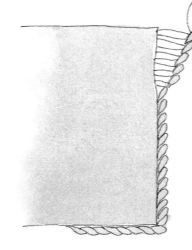

8 **Adding twisted cord to the edges by hand.** You could finish the cloth using a twisted cord. Take small stitches along the edge of the fabric. Let the needle catch the cord. Closely spaced stitches, worked with a matching thread, will make the join all but invisible.

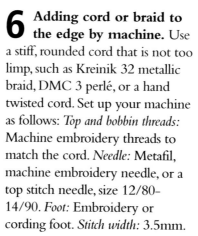

CHRISTMAS BOW

Bows and ribbons have a significant role in creating the festive atmosphere. This fabric Christmas bow is edged with wire-stiffened ribbon so that the bow can be shaped. Choose a ribbon colour to add a bright accent of colour to the bow fabric. If the wired ribbon cannot be found, use any beautiful ribbon that will complement the fabric.

1 Use spray starch to stiffen all the fabric. Fold the fabric in half, right sides facing each other, making a piece 11in (28cm) x 14in (36cm). Stitch around the edges leaving a gap at the top through which to turn the fabric.

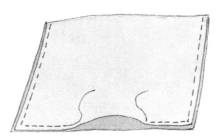

2 **Tie.** Fold the tie fabric into a piece measuring 4in (10cm) x 10in (25.5cm). Stitch, leaving a gap to turn it inside out. Turn all fabric pieces to the right side and iron the edges.

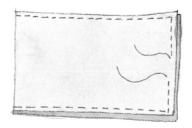

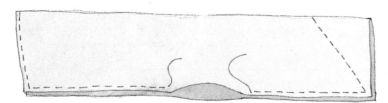

3 **Tails.** Fold the tail fabric into two pieces, 36in (92cm) x 5in (13cm). Stitch as indicated, again leaving a gap to turn the tail inside out. Turn the fabric to the right side and iron the edges.

4 **Adding wire ribbon.** Set up the machine as follows: *Stitch:* Zig-zag or straight stitch. *Needle:* Machine embroidery needle. *Thread:* Matching metallic thread. *Foot:* Embroidery or cording foot.

5 Place the ribbon under the fabric with the ribbon edge protruding. Pin in place. Allow ¼in (0.5cm) to show under the fabric. With a zig-zag stitch, stitch along the edge of the fabric. Apply ribbon to all visible edges of all the pieces.

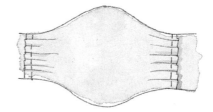

6 **Assembly.** Using your fingers, evenly gather the edges of the tie until they measure 2in (5cm) at the centre.

7 Lay the tie down with the wrong side uppermost. Place the bow on top of it. Bring the bottom of the tie up, and stitch it by hand to the back of the bow.

8 Position the tails so they are evenly spaced over the bottom portion of the tie. If necessary, they may be secured in position with pins. Turn the top edge of the tie over the tails, making sure you turn under the raw edge. Slip stitch the two together.

9 **To hang.** Sew a small curtain ring on the back of the tie, near the top. You can now, hang the bow from a picture hook or small panel pin, in a place of your choice.

THE
TASSELS

THE BASIC TASSEL

This provides the starting point for all the tassels in the book. Threads are wound around a card to build up the bulk of the tassel. They are then removed, and then wrapped to create an impressive decoration. You can use a range of coloured threads for a variety of attractive effects.

YOU WILL NEED

- [ ] 12 skeins of stranded embroidery cotton
- [ ] heavy mounting card 2 pieces about 5in (13cm) x 8in (20cm)
- [ ] tapestry needle
- [ ] cotton ball

NOTE

Before starting, consider the scale of a tassel. It should be such that it is in proportion with the object on which it is to be used. For instance, a small bag would be dwarfed by a large tassel. Tassels are greedy consumers of thread but don't skimp as a tassel can never be too fat. Allow an extra 1in (1.25cm) of tassel length to allow for final trimming.

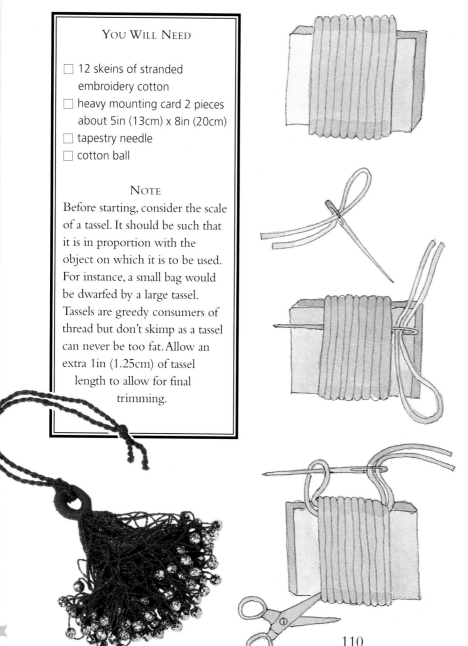

1 Wind thread around the 8in (20cm) dimension of the cards, or adjust the card size to suit your project. If using machine threads, wind 150-200 turns. With thicker hand embroidery threads, 50 winds will produce a nice plump shape. Do not pull the threads too tight. Remember that the top portion of threads will be used as the head.

2 Take a strand of thread about 4yds (3.7m) long, the same colour as the tassel, and fold it in half to create a loop. Pass the loop through the eye of the needle.

3 Pass the needle and thread under the wound threads at the top edge of the card, leaving the loop showing at one side and the needle at the other.

4 Pass the needle through the end of the loop and pull tight. If you are using fine or difficult threads, it may be necessary to tie the top securely before cutting. Cut through the threads at the bottom. Ease the threads from the card and secure with another stitch or two through the top.

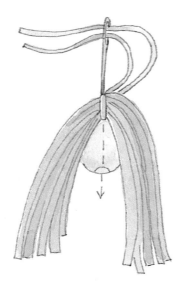

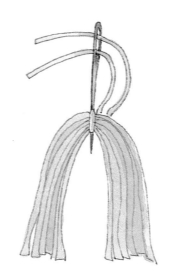

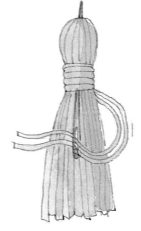

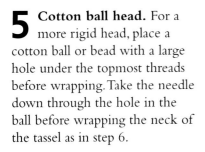

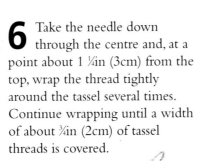

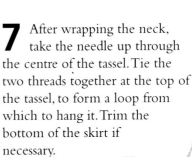

5 **Cotton ball head.** For a more rigid head, place a cotton ball or bead with a large hole under the topmost threads before wrapping. Take the needle down through the hole in the ball before wrapping the neck of the tassel as in step 6.

6 Take the needle down through the centre and, at a point about 1 ¼in (3cm) from the top, wrap the thread tightly around the tassel several times. Continue wrapping until a width of about ¾in (2cm) of tassel threads is covered.

7 After wrapping the neck, take the needle up through the centre of the tassel. Tie the two threads together at the top of the tassel, to form a loop from which to hang it. Trim the bottom of the skirt if necessary.

MULTI-COLOURED TASSEL

To create a tassel with a bright array of colours, simultaneously wind two or three different thread colours together on the card. To stop the balls or reels of coloured threads from tangling, try putting them in individual jars and pulling the thread through a large hole in the lid.

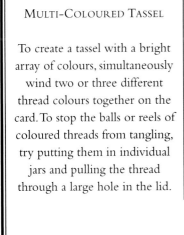

ORNATE TASSEL

An ornate tassel with great decorative appeal is easy to make and requires just a few extra steps beyond the basic tassel. Here an extra skirt is added, with detached buttonhole stitch worked on the head. Beads worked into the head and into the buttonhole stitch contribute to a rich-looking tassel.

1 Wind the first thread, a colour of your choice, around the cards as many times as needed to make a full skirt. Be generous with the thread. Cut the thread and secure it with small pieces of tape. This will form the under skirt. Choose a complementary thread colour for the next layer. Wrap this thread over the first bundle, again being generous. Make up the tassel following instructions for the basic tassel (pages 110–111).

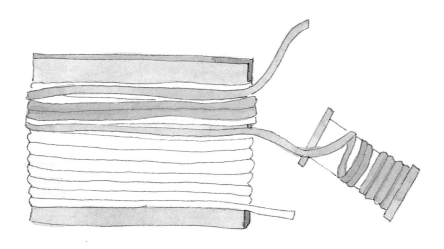

YOU WILL NEED

- [ ] 12 skeins of stranded embroidery cotton
- [ ] heavy mounting card 2 pieces about 5in (13cm) x 8in (20cm)
- [ ] tapestry needle
- [ ] cotton ball

2 Cut back the second thread colour, or overskirt. Use a ruler, if necessary, to make the overskirt follow an even line around the tassel. The overskirt may be trimmed to any length. If additional colours are wanted, just wrap your chosen colours around the card before making up the tassel, and cut back each colour to expose as much of each as is wanted.

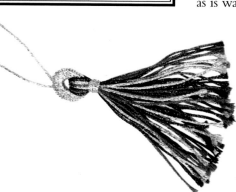

JINGLE BELL TASSEL

Padded tassel heads offer a secure anchor for threads that might be used to add other embellishments. A piece of rolled felt works extremely well. The padded centre offers an ideal place to finish off with hidden stitches when the heads are decorated with threads of several colours.

YOU WILL NEED

- ☐ 12 skeins of stranded embroidery cotton
- ☐ heavy mounting card 2 pieces about 5in (13cm) x 8in (20cm)
- ☐ tapestry needle
- ☐ rectangular strip of felt 1in (2.5cm) x 9in (23 cm)
- ☐ cord ¹⁄₁₆in (1.5mm)–⅛in (3mm) diameter
- ☐ large eye needle
- ☐ sewing needle
- ☐ dressmaker's thread
- ☐ bells

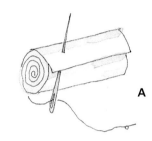

A

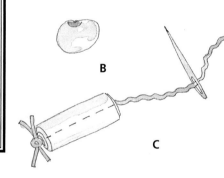

B

C

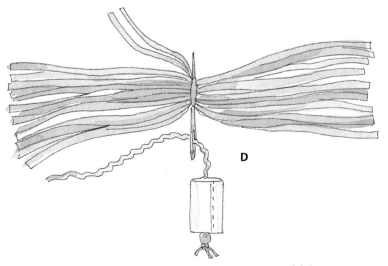

D

1 To incorporate the padding, make the basic tassel through steps 1-4, page 110. Instead of taking the needle down through the bundle of threads, leave the tying thread at the top of the tassel.

2 **Padding the head.** Cut a rectangular strip of felt 1in (2.5cm) x 9in (23cm). Roll up the strip very tightly and stitch along the edge (A). Take a couple of stitches across the ends to round them off. You could use a cotton ball instead (B).

3 To add an ornamental cord, make a twisted cord using matching colours of embroidery thread, or purchase a ready made cord of ¹⁄₁₆in (33mm)–⅛in (1.5mm) diameter. Knot the end of the cord and thread it through the eye of a large needle. Push the needle through the centre of the felt roll pulling the cord through (C).

4 Lay the tassel flat on a table. Using the needle carrying the cord which has been passed through the pad, pass the cord through the centre of the tassel (D). The pad should fit securely under the threads.

5 **Adding bells.** Before
wrapping the neck, add a
few bells to some of the threads
which make up the tassel body, or
feed some bells on to a separate
thread and pass it under the
tying threads.

6 Carefully pick up the tassel
and arrange and smooth the
threads over the felt pad. Take the
tying threads down through the
tassel and felt pad.

7 Bring the tying threads out
at the neck and wind them
around the tassel. Finish off the
tassel by stitching some loose
threads two or three times
through the side of the neck, as
inconspicuously as possible.
Thread a bead or ring through
the top cord for a nice finishing
effect. If you prefer a more
decorative tassel, work detached
buttonhole stitch over the head.

DECORATED TASSEL

To give the tassel head a more decorative appearance, detached buttonhole stitch can be worked over the top. This technique demands that the head of the tassel is made with a rolled felt pad, or with a cotton ball on the inside, giving the head sufficient substance to support the extra stitching.

YOU WILL NEED

- ☐ 12 skeins of DMC 5 perlé, assorted colours
- ☐ heavy mounting card 2 pieces about 5in (13cm) x 8in (20cm)
- ☐ tapestry needle
- ☐ rectangular strip of felt 1in (2.5cm) x 9in (23 cm)
- ☐ cord ¹⁄₁₆in (1.5mm)–¹⁄₈in (3mm) diameter
- ☐ large eye needle
- ☐ sewing needle
- ☐ dressmaker's thread
- ☐ curtain ring

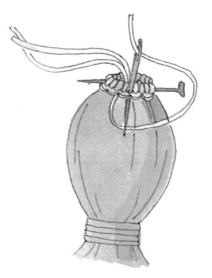

1 Make up a basic tassel with a padded head, following the jingle bells tassel, pages 114–115. Using either a small curtain ring or bolt washer ½in (1.25cm) diameter, work buttonhole stitch around the ring. Place the ring on the top of the tassel, passing the tassel's hanger threads through its centre, and pin in place while working.

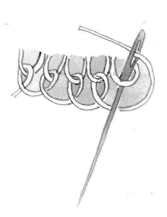

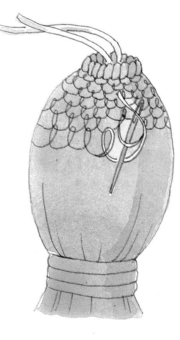

2 Working from the buttonhole stitch around the ring, use a tapestry needle with contrasting thread to continue working buttonhole stitch down over the tassel head. The first row is the most difficult to work. The technique becomes easier as you progress. The stitching will begin to look like a snug cap over the top of the tassel head. The detached buttonhole stitch is so called because it is not anchored to a background fabric. If the needle runs short of thread, a hidden stitch could be taken in the head to secure the tail of the working thread and the start of a new one.

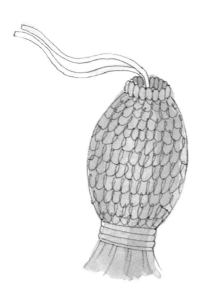

3 The detached buttonhole stitches should follow the contours of the tassel head. To do this, increase or decrease stitches as you work. Hold the cap in position by pinning it to the head of the tassel while working.

4 Finish off the last row when the neck of the tassel is reached. Take the needle through the body of the tassel head as the last row is worked, anchoring the cap securely in place.

BEADED TASSEL

Bead-encrusted tassel heads and hanging loops can add remarkable glitter and adornment to the decoration. The hanging loop will be strengthened at the same time as it is decorated. Beads are added as detached buttonhole stitch is worked over the threads, forming the loop.

YOU WILL NEED

- ☐ a selection of beads
- ☐ small needle that will pass through the beads
- ☐ dressmaker's thread
- ☐ craft foam board
- ☐ T-pins

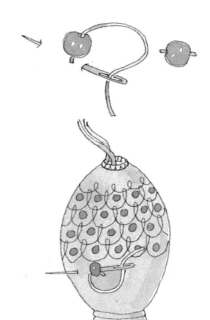

1 Beading the tassel head. For this technique, first make a basic tassel with a padded head, following the instructions for the jingle bells tassel, page 114–115.

2 Anchor the beading thread to the tassel head and thread on a single bead. Pass the needle back through the head and travel to the next bead position under the surface of the tassel head. Attach one bead at a time. Beads can be placed as near to or far from each other as desired. You could add them between the loops of detached buttonhole stitches.

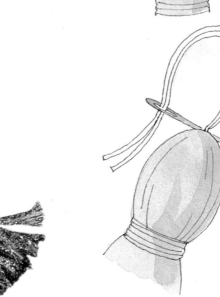

3 Adding beads to the hanging loop. The top of the tassel head will have two threads coming from it. These are intended to be used to hang the tassel. If these threads are too short, secure them with a few stitches and add a new one. Secure the added thread well with small stitches, so the tassel does not fall off once it is hanging. Make a loop. To finish off a thread, take the needle through the head, working downwards and then up, using small inconspicuous stitches.

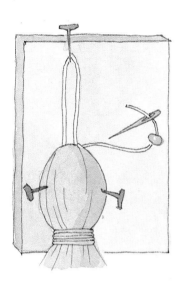

4 Pin the loop to a craft foam board with T-pins before you continue to work the tassel. You will find it much easier to work the buttonhole stitch over a taut thread than a loose one.

6 Work stitches around the loop, adding beads, randomly, as work progresses. When stitches have been worked, secure the thread inside the tassel head

5 Thread the needle with the thread selected for the buttonhole stitch. Add beads to this thread. Work the buttonhole stitch over the loop, securing the beads at each stitch.

RIBBON TASSEL WITH BELLS

Ribbon tassels make attractive Christmas decorations. Ribbons or cord add a special texture and look to the tassels. They can be embellished with the addition of beads, sequins, buttons, and other bits and pieces. Look in the small hardware section of your D.I.Y. shop for interesting bits.

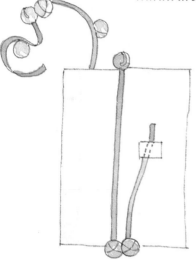

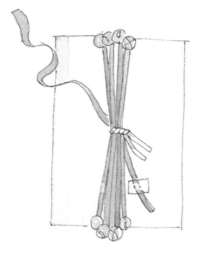

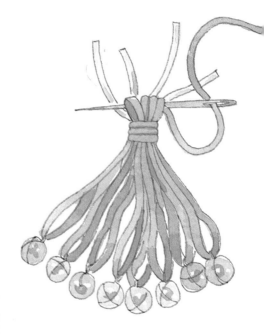

1 Thread all of the bells onto the ribbon. Tape one end of the ribbon to the card. Wrap it around the long side of the card, arranging it so that a bell falls at each edge on each wrap of the ribbon.

2 Once you've wrapped the ribbon, pinch it together at the centre of the card. Fix a twist-tie to secure it. Turn the card over, pinch the ribbon together, and fix another twist-tie.

3 Remove the tape and gently ease the ribbon off the card. Fold it so that the two twist-ties are together at the top of the tassel. Remember, the finished tassel will be half of the length of the ribbon as it was wrapped on the card.

4 Take the excess ribbon, and make a few wraps below the top of the tassel creating a neck. Thread the trailing ribbon into a needle, and take this through the wrapped neck. Remove the twist ties. Secure the tail of the ribbon at the top of the tassel. Make a loop from which to hang the tassel, and wrap the excess ribbon around the neck. Secure the final wrap of ribbon with a couple of firm stitches.

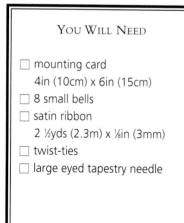

YOU WILL NEED

- [ ] mounting card
  4in (10cm) x 6in (15cm)
- [ ] 8 small bells
- [ ] satin ribbon
  2 ½yds (2.3m) x ⅛in (3mm)
- [ ] twist-ties
- [ ] large eyed tapestry needle

Fabric Tassels

Tassels made from fabric are easy and quick to make. Use any bright, shiny, fabric such as lamé, or patterned Christmas fabric. Use a combination of colours and patterns for a different effect. It is best to use a fabric that is not too prone to fraying.

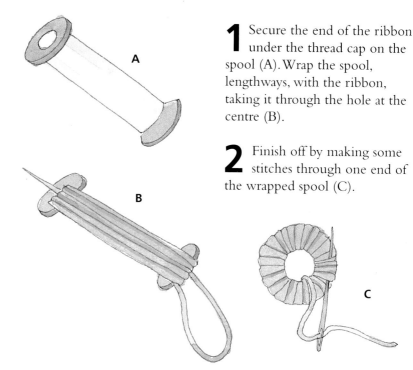

1 Secure the end of the ribbon under the thread cap on the spool (A). Wrap the spool, lengthways, with the ribbon, taking it through the hole at the centre (B).

2 Finish off by making some stitches through one end of the wrapped spool (C).

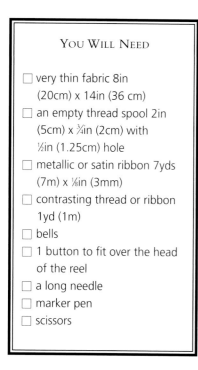

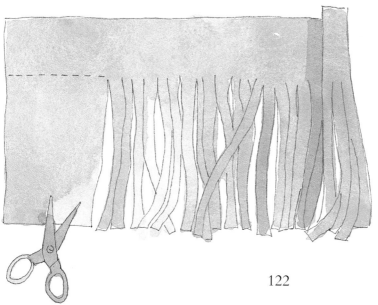

3 Take the fabric strip and mark a faint line 1 ¾in (4.5cm) along the top of it. Cut the fabric into ¼in (0.5cm) strips up to the marked line.

122

4 Roll the uncut fabric heading into a tight roll. Hold it securely with a few neat stitches.

5 Insert the rolled heading into the centre, at the bottom, of the wrapped reel. Make a loop from which to hang the tassel. Place a button or ring on top of the reel and pull the hanging loop through. Stitch the button to the wrapping on the reel with four holding stitches. Tie ribbon and ornaments around the waist of the tassel.

HEAVY FABRIC TASSELS

Tassels can be made from a heavier fabric, like felt. These are quick and simply made, and can be used the same way as all other tassels. To do this, cut a piece of fabric to the desired length. Mark a heading at the top, measuring down about one-third of the full length of the tassel. Cut the lower part into ¼in (0.5cm) strips, up to the mark. Roll it up tightly and tie with a ribbon, leather thong, or cord. Make a loop from which to attach or hang the tassel and secure it to the top of the tassel.

CONTRIBUTORS AND CREDITS

My special thanks to all who contributed their products and services for use in projects for this book including those previously mentioned; DMC Creative World Ltd, S.C.S. USA, Timber Lane Press North, Rainbow Gallery, YLI Corporation, Kreinik Manufacturing Co. Inc., and the companies listed below.

Sewing and machine embroidery threads
Perivale Gütermann Ltd
Wadsworth Road
Greenford
Middlesex, UB6 7JS

Ribbons
C.M. Offray & Son Ltd
Fir Tree Place
Church Road
Ashford
Middlesex, TW15 2PH

Non-woven interfacings, stabilizers
Freudenberg Non-wovens Ltd
The Vilene Corporation
P.O. Box 3
Greetland
Halifax, HX4 8NJ

Needlework, art, and craft supplies
Ben Franklin Crafts
1487 Midway Blvd
Oak Harbor
WA 98277

Supply of PFAFF sewing machine
PFAFF (Britain)
91 Coleman Road
Leicester, LE5 4LE

Supply of PFAFF sewing machine
PFAFF American Sales Corp.
610 Winters Ave
Paramus
NJ 07653

Supply of Bernina sewing machine
Northwest Sewing
6414 Roosevelt Way
N.E Seattle
Washington

The following artists have contributed their talents and skills to the design, stitching and making up of the projects listed. To them, I offer my heartfelt thanks.

Origami Bags and Decorations
Glenda Scott – *design and make up*
Gail Harker – *stitching*

Teddy Bear Stocking, Nine Drummers Drumming, Ten Pipers Piping
Nancy Morrill – *design and stitching*

Small Christmas Containers
June Kendell – *make up*
Gail Harker – *design*

Christmas Bow
Caroline Burton – *stitching and make up*
Gail Harker – *design*

Buttonhole Rings, Tassels on Buttonhole Rings
Mary Stoll – *stitching*
Gail Harker – *design and stitching*

Christmas Rose Cushion, Christmas Rose Photo Frame, Poinsettia Book Covers and Book Marks
Linda Downing – *design, make up and stitching*

Buttons, Beads, Sequins
Gail Harker – *design and stitching*
Mary Stoll – *stitching*

Christmas Tree Skirt, Cardinal Points Tablecloth, Circular Tablecloth
Alba Romeo –*stitching and make up*
Gail Harker – *design*

Glittering Decorations★
Gail Harker – *design and stitching*

★ Some glittering decorations were stitched by the staff of the Ben Franklin Store, Oak Harbor, Washington, USA

All other projects were designed and stitched by Gail Harker

SUPPLIERS

The following companies are distributors or suppliers of the products listed in the projects.

USA

Rainbow Gallery
7412 Fulton Ave
North Hollywood, CA 91605
Neon rays and a large selection of unusual embroidery threads

S.C.S. USA
9631 N.E.
Colfax Portland
Oregon, 97220-1232
Tel: 1-800-547-8025
Madeira machine embroidery threads, other needlework and craft supplies

Kreinik Manufacturing Co. Inc
3106 Timanus Lane
Suite 101
Baltimore, MD 21244
Kreinik metallic braids

Timber Lane Press
North 22700
Rim Rock
Hayden Lake
Idaho 83835
USA Timtex interfacing

YLI Corporation
482 North Freedom Blvd
Provo, Utah, 84601
YLI silk ribbons

Herrshners Inc
2800 Hoover Road
Stevens Point
WI 54492–0001
Tel: 1-800-441-0838

United Kingdom

Mace & Nairn
89 Crane Street
Salisbury
Wilts, SP1 2PY
Tel: 01722 416 397
Wide variety of needlework supplies including cotton balls and mail order

The Silver Thimble
The Old Malt House
Clarence Street
Bath
Avon, BA1 5NS
Tel: 01225 423457
Rainbow Gallery threads, and other needlework supplies

Heritage Stitchcraft
Redbrook Lane
Brerton
Nr Rugeley
Staffordshire, WS15 1QV
Tel: 01889 575256
YLI silk ribbons, and other needlework supplies

John Lewis
278-306 Oxford Street
London, W1A 1EX
Tel: 0171 629 7711
Ribbons, threads, fabric, and blind stiffener

DMC Creative World Ltd
Pullman Road
Wigston
Leicester, LE8 2DY
Tel: 0116 2811040
Threads, fabrics and other needlework supplies

Coats Patons Crafts
P.O. Box McMullen Road
Darlington
Co. Durham, DL1 1YQ
Kreinik metallic braids and ribbons

Australia

Down Under
Suite 3
559 Sydney Road
Seaforth
N.S.W. 2092
Rainbow Gallery threads, and other needlework supplies

Cotton Creations
P.O. Box 804
Epping
N.S.W. 2121
Silk ribbons, and other needlework supplies

Ireland Needlecrafts
Unit 4, 2-4 Keppel Drive
Hallam, Victoria 3803
Kreinik metallic braids

New Zealand

Margaret Barrett D.I.S.T. Ltd
P.O Box 12-034
19 Beasley Ave
Penrose, Auckland
Silk ribbons, and other needlework supplies

Greville Parker
286 Queens Street
Masterton
Kreinik metallic braids

INDEX

BRITISH AND AMERICAN EMBROIDERY TERMS

British	American
Cotton perlé	Pearl cotton
Stranded cotton – any number of strands	Six-strand-embroidery floss – could be any number of strands
Coton à broder	Brilliant cutwork and embroidery thread
Soft embroidery cotton	Matte embroidery cotton
Hoop (rarely used)	Hoop – round embroidery hoop only
Frame – any frame to hold embroidery, round, square, or rectangular.	Frame – any shape for holding embroidery other than round
Tacking	Basting
Wadding	Batting
Drawing pin	Thumbtack